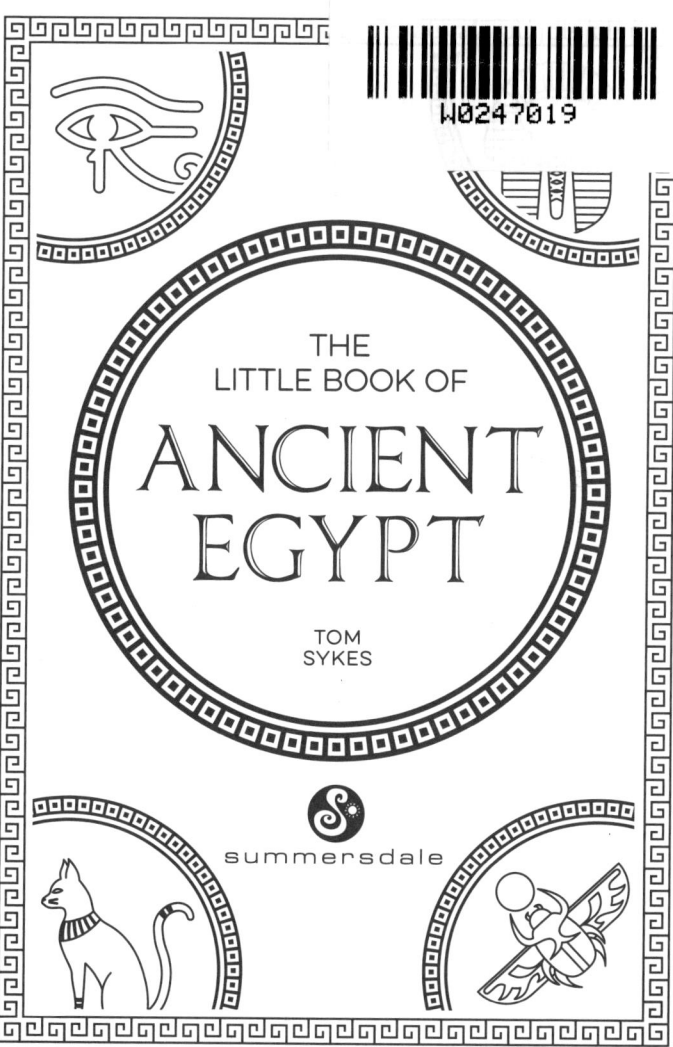

THE
LITTLE BOOK OF

ANCIENT EGYPT

TOM
SYKES

summersdale

THE LITTLE BOOK OF ANCIENT EGYPT

An Hachette UK Company
www.hachette.co.uk

Summersdale Publishers
Part of Octopus Publishing Group Limited
Carmelite House
50 Victoria Embankment
LONDON
EC4Y 0DZ
UK

www.summersdale.com

This FSC® label means that materials and other controlled sources used for the product have been responsibly sourced

FSC
www.fsc.org

MIX
Paper | Supporting responsible forestry
FSC® C018236

The authorized representative in the EEA is Hachette Ireland, 8 Castlecourt Centre, Dublin 15, D15 XTP3, Ireland (email: info@hbgi.ie)

Printed and bound in Poland

ISBN: 978-1-83799-691-9
eISBN: 978-1-83799-692-6

Substantial discounts on bulk quantities of Summersdale books are available to corporations, professional associations and other organizations. For details contact general enquiries: telephone: +44 (0) 1243 771107 or email: enquiries@summersdale.com.

THE LITTLE BOOK OF ANCIENT ROME

Tom Sykes

ISBN: 978-1-83799-561-5

The Ancient Roman civilization has captured human imagination for generations. Discover the key events, people and trivia you need to know to understand this remarkable period of history.

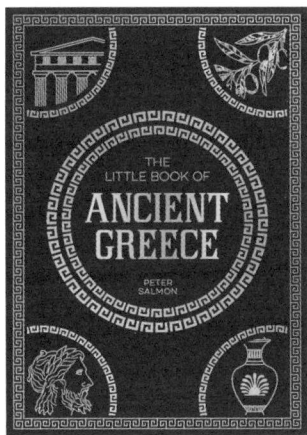

THE LITTLE BOOK OF ANCIENT GREECE

Peter Salmon

ISBN: 978-1-83799-535-6

The echoes of the Ancient Greeks can still be heard, loud and clear, today. From warfare and politics, to art, culture and everyday life, uncover their history with this fascinating little book.

Have you enjoyed this book?
If so, find us on Facebook at
Summersdale Publishers,
on Twitter/X at **@Summersdale**
and on Instagram, TikTok and Bluesky
at **@summersdalebooks** and get
in touch. We'd love to hear from you!

WWW.SUMMERSDALE.COM

Image Credits

Central cover circle © Ana Lo/Shutterstock.com;
Border © Omeris/Shutterstock.com;
Pharaoh, scarab beetle, eye of Horus © imhaf maulana/Shutterstock.com;
Cat – pp.3, 5, 139 © WinWin artlab/Shutterstock.com;
Pyramids – pp.7, 19, 26, 39, 41, 73, 76, 85, 93, 105, 109
© imhaf maulana/Shutterstock.com

CONTENTS

INTRODUCTION

Almost 2,000 years after its demise, Ancient Egypt continues to capture our imaginations. While this may largely be due to pop culture images of enigmatic pyramids, sphinxes, mummies and curses, it's worth remembering that Ancient Egyptian civilization was strikingly unique and progressive in myriad ways.

Compared to other societies before and since, Egypt granted freedoms to women, who could own property, get divorced, and work as doctors, clerics and merchants. They could ascend to the highest post of all, as the mighty pharaohs Merneith, Nefertiti and Cleopatra attest. Some might think that animal rights and protections are a recent development, yet the Greek historian Herodotus, when visiting Egypt in the fifth century BCE, was impressed by the near-equality to humans that sacred creatures (including cats, dogs and crocodiles) enjoyed.

As this book will divulge, Egypt also blazed trails in technology, engineering, medicine, mathematics,

literature, art, architecture, agriculture, administration and politics, shaping the modern societies we live in today.

Egypt's extraordinary culture deserves to be more widely known, since it is often sidelined by our modern emphasis on Greece and Rome. So prepare for a trip back through the mists of time.

AN
INTRODUCTION
TO ANCIENT EGYPT

Historians mark Ancient Egypt's origins
from around 5000 BCE, when two polities in
the southern regions of the River Nile – Upper
Egypt and Lower Egypt – were unified into a
powerful civilization. At its zenith, in 1550–1070
BCE, Ancient Egypt covered 380,000–500,000
square miles. The civilization underwent several
stages of development: the Predynastic Period,
the Early Dynastic Period, the Old Kingdom,
the First Intermediate Period, the Middle
Kingdom, the Second Intermediate Period, the
New Kingdom, the Third Intermediate Period,
the Late Period and the Ptolemaic Kingdom.

In this chapter we'll explore the key events
and personalities that shaped Ancient Egypt
and made it so fascinating for us today.

ANCIENT EGYPT: A TIMELINE

Before we delve into the details, the following timeline should serve as an overview of Ancient Egypt's rise and fall.

Note: Given the paucity of reliable primary sources – especially from the Old Kingdom era – there is some disagreement among Egyptologists about the most accurate chronology for Ancient Egypt. This timeline draws upon the Conventional Egyptian chronology, on which most scholars agree. The broad dating of periods is Professor Ian Shaw's, as proposed in *The Oxford History of Ancient Egypt* (2000), and is approximate, as are most of the dates for specific events in this book.

PREDYNASTIC PERIOD

5000–4000 BCE – The Nile Valley region spawns various cultures, of which the earliest known are the Badarians. They domesticate animals, practise agriculture and produce ornate redware (pottery made from iron-rich clay).

4000–3200 BCE – The Naqada culture builds significant settlements in Gerzeh and El-Amrah and forges trade links with Nubia and Mesopotamia. It makes breakthroughs

in symbolic writing, which would later influence hieroglyphics, and in the use of flint and copper tools.

3200–3150 BCE – The final phase of Naqada development sees the emergence of powerful monarchs leading large, hierarchical polities.

EARLY DYNASTIC PERIOD

3150 BCE – Legend credits Narmer (aka Menes, see page 16) as the pharaoh who unifies the civilizations of Upper Egypt, which stretches from south of the Nile River delta to Aswan, and those of Lower Egypt, comprising the Nile Delta and lands as far north as the Mediterranean Sea. For this reason, pharaoh means "ruler of two lands".

3150–2686 BCE – Egypt expands its territory by colonizing lower Nubia (which includes parts of modern-day Egypt and Sudan) and southern Canaan (comprising areas of what is today Palestine, Israel and Jordan). Many of the defining characteristics of Ancient Egyptian culture originate from this time, such as grand administrative buildings, temples, hieroglyphics, the widespread use of copper, and unique arts and crafts including pottery.

OLD KINGDOM

2686–2494 BCE – The Third and Fourth dynasties see the construction of some of the grandest pyramids, including the Saqqara necropolis where, among other royalty, the pharaohs Djoser (who reigned around 2686–2649 BCE) and his son Djoserty (2649–2643 BCE) are buried. Architects under King Sneferu (2613–2589 BCE) are credited with devising the "smooth-sided" pyramids, the most iconic of which are in the Giza Plateau. In Sneferu's reign Egypt enters a golden age in which the civilization spreads as far as parts of Nubia in the south, Libya in the west and Sinai in the east.

2494–2181 BCE – During the Fifth and Sixth dynasties, and particularly under the reigns of Sahure (12–13 years in power; dates uncertain) and Isesi (33–44 years of reign), Egypt makes huge progress in commerce, war, administration and religious reform. Profitable commodities such as slaves, myrrh, copper, gold and cedar trees are acquired from the Levantine coast and the mysterious Land of Punt (now Ethiopia or Somalia), while there are victories over kingdoms in Lebanon and Libya and the period sees the creation of a faster, more efficient navy.

FIRST INTERMEDIATE PERIOD

2181–2125 BCE – Often referred to as Egypt's dark age, a political schism occurs between the Old and Middle kingdoms. After the Sixth Dynasty, Egypt fragments into competing power bases in Thebes (Upper Egypt) and Herakleopolis (Lower Egypt). There is an economic slump and regional governors (nomarchs) start to siphon power from the pharaohs. While fewer larger buildings are constructed, there are leaps forward in smaller-scale arts and crafts, especially sculpture and tomb art. The famous didactic literary work *Instruction for Merikare* emerges at this time.

THE MIDDLE KINGDOM

2125–1773 BCE – In many ways a golden age of prosperity and stability, when the pharaohs conquer further territory in Nubia and expand trade with Punt and the Levant. The pharaoh Mentuhotep II (reign: 2055–2004 BCE) reunifies Egypt and lays the groundwork for its future successes. Innovations in irrigation and agriculture, especially in the Fayum region, aid population growth, while architectural standouts include the Pyramid of Senusret III and its elaborate burial complex. Under the 45-year rule of Amenemhat II (dates uncertain), Egypt massively increases its mining operations for copper and turquoise.

SECOND INTERMEDIATE PERIOD

1773–1550 BCE – The Thirteenth Dynasty cedes control of northern Egypt to the Hyksos, an advanced people from modern-day Israel, Palestine and Syria. Southern Egypt remains under Egyptian rule, its capital in Thebes, and the pharaohs Seqenenre Tao, Kamose and Ahmose I pursue a protracted war against the Hyksos. Ahmose I oversees the most ambitious construction projects since the Middle Kingdom, including the last pyramid to be erected by an Egyptian ruler at Abydos. The Hyksos are finally defeated at the Siege of Avaris (1550 BCE) and expelled from the Nile Delta area.

NEW KINGDOM OF EGYPT

1550–1069 BCE – In Egypt's heyday, the New Kingdom builds astonishing structures such as the temples at Karnak, the Valley of the Kings and the rock-cut temples of Abu Simbel. Pharaohs come to be seen as divine rulers and expand the empire with military victories over the Hittites (from what is now Turkey) and populations in Nubia, Libya and western Asia. In 1274 BCE, Ramses II wins the Battle of Kadesh against the Hittite monarch Muwatalli II, the first properly recorded battle in history.

THIRD INTERMEDIATE PERIOD

945–664 BCE – After the New Kingdom is destroyed by internal strife and piratical raids by the Sea Peoples, Egypt breaks up into smaller monarchies in Delta, Thebes and Lower Egypt, which is ruled by the Libyan dynasties (twenty-fourth to twenty-second centuries BCE). The Nubian Kushites reunite Egypt between 715 and 664 BCE, the Twenty-fifth Dynasty, but this doesn't stop further incursions by the Sea Peoples and, later, the Assyrians.

LATE PERIOD

664–305 BCE – The Late Period begins with Neo-Assyrians indirectly ruling Egypt and, in 525 BCE, the Persians under Cyrus the Great colonize the territory. During the Twenty-eighth and Thirtieth dynasties, Egyptians achieve short-lived independence before again falling under Persian control. Alexander the Great conquers Egypt in 332 BCE, introducing the Ptolemaic dynasty under the general Ptolemy I Soter, who hails from Macedon in Greece. Under the Saite pharaohs, who reign throughout most of the Late Period, Egypt enjoys a renaissance, with these foreign civilizations introducing new technologies, customs and artistic styles.

THE PTOLEMAIC KINGDOM

305–30 BCE – Ptolemy I Soter (reign: 305–282 BCE) secures his personal hegemony over Egypt when, after the collapse of Alexander's empire, he defeats rivals in the Wars of the Diadochi and Alexander's successor and former bodyguard Perdiccas. The Ptolemaic dynasty rules with an iron fist, repressing and heavily taxing the populace. But it is also culturally enlightened: Ptolemy II Philadelphus (280–247 BCE) builds the Library of Alexandria and the Pharos lighthouse, one of the Seven Wonders of the Ancient World.

In this era there is immense Greek-Egyptian hybridity, with new gods blending the attributes of old ones, and the capital city, Alexandria, showcasing Greek rationality and Egyptian mysticism. The cunning and ruthless Cleopatra VII, the last Ptolemaic monarch, allies with Julius Caesar and Mark Antony in their struggles for Roman succession but is ultimately overthrown by Octavian (the future Emperor Augustus). In 30 BCE, Egypt ceases to be a sovereign state and becomes a province of the Roman Empire.

WHERE IT ALL STARTED

In the Predynastic Period, small nomadic communities started to settle in and farm the Nile Valley. The river's yearly floods made the land fertile, supporting barley, wheat and flax growth. These populations also developed animal husbandry, raising mainly sheep, cattle and goats.

Sophisticated cultures emerged in Upper Egypt. The Badarians (4400–4000 BCE) pioneered pottery and basic social organization, while the Naqada (4000–3100 BCE) were adroit at metalworking and commerce. Their burial practices involved elaborate tomb-building, which influenced later Egyptian funerary architecture.

These predynastic polities were soon trading with the Levant, Nubia and Mesopotamia (contemporary Iraq and parts of bordering countries). Religious rituals and political structures became formalized, prefiguring the Egypt of the pharaohs.

BURIED INSIGHTS

In the 1920s and 1930s CE, Sir Alan Gardiner's team discovered the Badarians' graveyards, built around 4400–4000 BCE. The wrought pottery, ivory statues and other grave goods hugely expanded our understanding of this era.

AN ELUSIVE TRAILBLAZER

The pharaoh Narmer, his name meaning "raging catfish" or a variation of that phrase, is credited with having unified Upper and Lower Egypt into a powerful civilization in 3150 BCE. Narmer, in his role as the gods' representative among mortals, established religious and political structures that would dominate Ancient Egypt for the rest of its existence. He was also likely the first pharaoh whose name appeared inside a serekh, a prestigious ceremonial frame that from his time onwards incorporated the names of Egyptian royalty. Narmer also expanded Egypt's borders, conquering rebellious tribes in the Nile Valley, and his tomb at Abydos, once strewn with shards of votive pots, is an impressive sight.

What we know of Narmer comes from archaeological finds including the Narmer Palette, uncovered by British Egyptologists in 1897–8 CE. However, there remains controversy among scholars as to whether Narmer was in fact another ruler entirely, called Menes, or whether these are two different names for the same man or Menes was Narmer's son and successor. Whoever Narmer really was, there is no doubting his – or someone else of that time's – influence over the future course of Egyptian civilization.

CONSOLIDATOR OF CONTROL

The pharaoh Djoser, who reigned in the Third Dynasty, kicked off the Old Kingdom during which architecture and religious customs flourished. Djoser created new trade routes and reinforced the kingdom's borders. Hieroglyphics show that he probably fought and defeated tribes in the Sinai Peninsula to secure resources like copper and turquoise.

In Djoser's time, the office of the pharaoh became holy and all-powerful. Thus, he was known by his Horus name, Netjerikhet, meaning "divine of body".

PYRAMID PIONEER

The pharaoh Djoser commissioned the step pyramid at Saqqara (about 19 miles south of modern Cairo), where he was also buried. It is thought to be the first mega-monument ever constructed. At 62 m (205 feet) high, it comprised six mastabas (flat roofs with sloping sides) and marked the transition in Egyptian architecture from the use of mud bricks to hardier limestone. It was the tallest building in the world for at least 40 years.

PYRAMIDS AND OTHER GREAT EDIFICES

Say "Ancient Egypt" to anyone and they'll likely think of the pyramids of the Old Kingdom. As pharaohs came to be regarded as divine figures, their tombs had to be suitably grand and prepare them for the afterlife.

Pharaoh Sneferu (c. 2600 BCE) is credited with constructing the first fully smooth-sided pyramid, the Red Pyramid at Dahshur. His earlier attempts, the Bent Pyramid and the Meidum Pyramid, had structural weaknesses and angular oddities – but lessons were learned from these errors.

The most iconic pyramids of all, those at Giza, emerged during the reigns of Khufu, Khafre and Menkaure. Still ranked as one of the Seven Wonders of the Ancient World, Khufu's Great Pyramid of Giza, was originally 146.6 m (481 feet) tall and required over 2 million blocks of limestone. Khafre built the world-famous Great Sphinx, a statue of a mythical beast with the body of a lion and the head of a man. The Sphinx was seen as a symbol of the pharaoh himself.

The pyramid where Menkaure was laid to rest was smaller and less grand, though is acclaimed for its innovative use of granite casing.

Both the Giza structures and Djoser's step pyramid were sited in Memphis, the bustling capital city of the Old Kingdom, at the heart of the Nile Delta. At its height, in the late Old Kingdom or early New Kingdom, Memphis was the nerve centre of Egyptian commerce, politics, religion and learning, and home to 100,000–200,000 people.

In addition to pyramids, Memphis boasted elaborate temple complexes and the largest statues ever carved in the civilization. The Temple of Ptah was likely begun in the Early Dynastic Period in tribute to the pre-eminent god of the Egyptians and was developed throughout the rest of Ancient Egypt's days. Sadly, there's little of it left today.

The pyramid trend declined in the Fifth and Sixth dynasties (2494–2181 BCE), with smaller versions at Abusir and Saqqara constructed cheaply, quickly and with inferior materials. That said, the cultural centrality of pyramids to Egyptians endured with the emergence of the Pyramid Texts (see page 21).

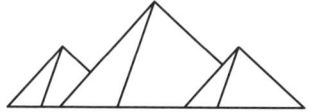

A TALENTED ALL-ROUNDER

Imhotep was the genius reputed to have designed Djoser's step pyramid. But he was something of a Renaissance man before the term existed, as demonstrated by his dictum "He who seeks knowledge, will find it." Imhotep was also a respected philosopher, scribe and doctor. Historians have deduced that he knew how to set broken bones, could perform surgical procedures, and understood symptoms of disease and the rudiments of infection (see page 108).

He seems to have been thought of highly during his life and long after. Imhotep's influence was international, with the Ancient Greeks binding him to Asclepius, their god of medicine. In the Late Period of Ancient Egypt, a whole millennium after he died, he was turned into the deity of wisdom and healing. It's hard to think of a greater compliment than that.

AHEAD OF HIS TIME

The contemporary science writer Siddhartha Mukherjee claims that Imhotep produced the oldest written diagnosis of cancer. Was there any treatment for the malady, in Imhotep's view? His answer: "There is none."

THE ROUGH GUIDE TO DEATH

Carved in hieroglyphics on pyramid walls – especially Saqqara's – during the Fifth and Sixth dynasties, the enigmatic Pyramid Texts are considered some of the oldest sacred writings on Earth. They were effectively spells, prayers, songs and incantations used to guide and smooth the transition of the pharaohs to the afterlife.

If the Pyramid Texts were properly recited and interpreted then the pharaoh's soul would be protected as it journeyed to the next world and, eventually, attained resurrection. Some of the writings suggest that the soul could physically travel into space and even transform into a star or other celestial body. Others claim that the deceased monarch could enjoy eternal life among the gods, merge with the sun deity Ra and even soar around the cosmos in his solar barque (flying ship). These cosmic and astronomical images were later to feed alternative histories of and conspiracy theories about Ancient Egypt (see pages 135–6).

The Pyramid Texts prefigured the later Coffin Texts and the *Egyptian Book of the Dead*, which extended its ideas and paradigms to non-royal Egyptians.

BREAKING THE LIMESTONE CEILING

Hatshepsut (1507–1458 BCE) was one of Egypt's most remarkable female pharaohs, with her reign occurring during the Eighteenth Dynasty (1550–1295 BCE). Shrewd, visionary and determined, she wanted to be judged on equal terms with any male monarch, prompting her to wear a false beard and insist on being depicted with a muscular, masculine body.

Her first taste of power was when she served as regent for her stepson, Thutmose III, who came to the throne aged just two and was deemed too young to rule. She kept him on the sidelines and ascended to the position of pharaoh, constructing the splendid Temple of Hatshepsut at Deir el-Bahari, near the Valley of the Kings. This spectacular mortuary temple was built into the cliffs and illustrated with scenes from Hatshepsut's reign, which is remembered for unprecedented peace, economic growth and cultural evolution. On Hatshepsut's watch, Egyptians made an expedition to the Land of Punt and brought back baboons, leopards and possibly giraffes, and exotic goods such as myrrh and incense were imported.

THE NAPOLEON OF EGYPT

Unlike his stepmother, Thutmose III (1479–1425 BCE) favoured military imperialism to advance his civilization. Later dubbed the "Napoleon of Egypt", he led 17 victorious campaigns against Canaanite and Mitanni city states in what is now North Africa and the Middle East.

Thutmose also commissioned some remarkable temples such as Karnak, renowned for its 134 columns, its Avenue of Sphinxes and 30 m tall obelisk. Thutmose proposed the sun god Amun-Ra as Egypt's divine protector, cementing his own power as pharaoh and shaping the city of Thebes as Egypt's religious hub.

By Thutmose's death, Ancient Egypt had grown to be the richest and biggest it would ever be, its territory spreading from Sudan in the south to the Euphrates River in the north.

HIS SOFTER SIDE

Thutmose was a keen botanist and erected one of the world's first botanical gardens at Karnak. After a successful military expedition, he would bring back exotic plants and animals in addition to captured slaves and loot.

THE BATTLE OF MEGIDDO

Thutmose III's tactical genius won the Battle of Megiddo in 1457 BCE, one of the most dramatic military contests of ancient times. Against the advice of his generals, Thutmose sent his highly disciplined and professional army through the Aruna Pass, in a region of what is now Israel, leaving it vulnerable to the forces of the Canaanite King Kadesh of Megiddo. Thutmose's high-risk strategy was to put his troops into a good position for an ambush.

Thutmose then pulled off a series of tactical masterstrokes. With infantrymen moving to the middle of the formation and chariots taking the flanks, the Egyptians scattered the Canaanites, with survivors fleeing back to the well-fortified city of Megiddo. Thutmose bided his time and laid siege to Megiddo, and Kadesh's men surrendered after seven months. To ensure future fealty from members of the Megiddo elite, Thutmose took their friends and relatives hostage.

The battle was recorded in detail by inscriptions on the walls of the Temple of Amun at Karnak. The victory marked Egypt's flowering into a true empire, achieving dominance over the Levant.

EGYPT'S RENAISSANCE

The social and political cohesion of the Middle Kingdom made for huge progress in the arts, crafts and the life of the mind. It was a gilded age for writing, with steps forward in both storytelling and philosophy. Standout works include the *Tale of Sinuhe*, about a court official who is exiled to Syria, and the *Instructions of Amenemhat*, which examined themes such as loyalty, forgiveness, wisdom and fate.

The Eloquent Peasant promoted *maat* (order and justice) by relating the narrative of a pauper who uses his oratory skills to win back his possessions that have been stolen by a corrupt official. In the Old Kingdom, literature had been preoccupied with the monarchy but now it related more to ordinary people.

Sculpture took a more naturalistic turn, focusing on the human body and away from the symbolism typical of the Old Kingdom. Depictions of the pharaohs and members of the elite included facial lines and expressions, foregrounding their humanity yet retaining their holy aspect. The statue of Amenemhat II is a classic example of this new style.

Similarly, architecture started to incorporate scenes of daily life, emphasizing the connection between

the godly and the everyday. Officials now preferred to be buried in rock-cut tombs rather than pyramids. An exemplar of such a tomb is Beni Hasan, on the eastern bank of the Nile, remarkable for its painted wall reliefs showing wrestling, military training and Egyptian merchants trading with Asians.

Pharaohs such as Amenemhat I and Senusret I erected beautiful pyramids, although these were not as ostentatious as those of the Old Kingdom as tastes became humbler.

Religion, too, was less restrictive and elitist in the Middle Kingdom, with the worship of Osiris meaning that the afterlife could be accessed by all, not just the upper classes. Coffin texts became available to the scribe and artisan classes, ensuring their safe passage to the next world. Smaller cults proliferated due to greater official tolerance of diverse attitudes to spirituality among Egyptians in all walks of life.

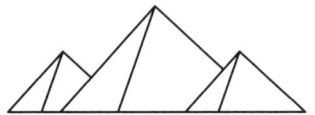

RELIGIOUS REVOLUTIONS

The New Kingdom saw a veritable revolution in religious beliefs and practices. Faith had always been an essential component of Egyptian life, but now its articulation and understanding were altering radically, and new deities were coming to prominence.

Amun, the god of Thebes, started to be associated more closely with the sun deity Ra during the reigns of pharaohs Amenhotep I and Thutmose I. Grand temples, Karnak being one of them, were erected in Amun's honour across Egypt, and the priests serving him attained vast wealth and political influence.

A CRAZY, MIXED-UP GOD

It's a paradox that, despite Amun being one of the most popular deities of the New Kingdom epoch, he was known as "the hidden one" due to his elusiveness. He was also dubbed "the great cackler" on account of sometimes being pictured with – and sounding like – a goose. Not a hugely respectable trait for such a powerful deity to possess, perhaps.

Pharaoh Akhenaten (1353–1336 BCE) made an enormous impact on the spiritual life of his subjects when he doggedly promoted the exclusive worship of the Aten deity (meaning "sun disc"). This effectively ushered in monotheism, the belief in only one god. Soon enough, devotion to other, lesser gods was outlawed and their temples shut down. Akhenaten moved Egypt's capital to Akhetaten (nowadays Tell el-Amarna), which became the epicentre of Aten adulation.

Akhenaten's successors Tutankhamun and Ay reversed his reforms, bringing back polytheism and Amun worshipping. They also abandoned Akhetaten and left it to ruin. In the latter days of the New Kingdom, the cult of Osiris became ever more vital to beliefs around death and resurrection. This prompted a tendency among Egyptians towards personal salvation, since Osiris promised that leading a good and just life would secure anyone, rich or poor, passage to the afterlife. Egyptians would express their love for Osiris and other gods in a more individual way, using amulets and prayers rather than through flamboyant public rituals.

BOLDNESS AND BEAUTY

Nefertiti (1370–1330 BCE) was Akhenaten's "Great Royal Wife", the title given to an Egyptian consort. However, she was no shrinking violet, instrumental as she was in her husband's radical new policies around spirituality, publicly and vehemently promoting Atenism. Historians debate whether she briefly reigned after Akhenaten's death.

Nefertiti's public impact may also have been due to her physical beauty. This is reflected in her celebrated limestone and painted stucco bust, discovered in the ruins of Akhetaten in 1912 CE. Now on display in Berlin, this 48 cm (19 in) tall and 20 kg (44 lbs) artwork is one of the most important relics of Ancient Egypt, symbolizing Nefertiti's grace and royal standing.

MUMMY OR NOT?

One theory is that Nefertiti is one of the mummies discovered in 1817 CE in KV21 (assigned by archaeologists and referring to the twenty-first tomb of the Kings' Valley) in the Valley of the Kings. More recent DNA analysis has been inconclusive as to the identity of the long-dead woman, but her left arm was placed across her chest in the classic Egyptian monarchical pose.

A VERY IMPORTANT JOURNEY

Ancient Egypt played a key part in the story of another great monotheistic religion and culture, that of the Jews. According to the Book of Exodus in the Hebrew Bible, despite their king Joseph initially enjoying good relations with the pharaohs, the Israelites were enslaved by the Egyptians during either the early New Kingdom or the Second Intermediate Period.

Their labour was essential to constructing the Nile Delta metropolises of Pithom and Ramses. The Bible recounts the liberation of the Israelites by the prophet Moses, who had the blessing of their all-powerful god Yahweh. Moses led his people out of Egypt and 400 km (250 miles) to the shores of the Dead Sea and the "promised land". Traditionally Jews date the origin of their culture to their settlement of this region, which is now, broadly speaking, Israel.

Though there is no clinching archaeological evidence for this version of events (speculated to have happened between 1290 and 1250 BCE), various inscriptions and steles (monuments marking graves and boundaries) uncovered in the region have suggested there is some truth to it.

ALMIGHTY GO-BETWEENS

As Amun worship mushroomed during the New Kingdom, so did the Theban High Priests of Amun. They were at their most powerful, both in terms of religious and political sway, in the Eighteenth Dynasty under the administrations of pharaohs Thutmose III and Amenhotep III.

They were tasked with presiding over the rituals and sacrifices to Amun at the Temple of Karnak, and running the plush estates and temples associated with the deity. Appointed by the pharaoh, the high priest was regarded as the liaison between the pharaoh and the gods. Whereas previously in Egyptian history the authority of the nomarchs (regional governors) would benefit from a weakened monarchy, by the end of the Eighteenth Dynasty it was the Amun clergy that increasingly threatened pharaonic power. Akhenaten possibly moved his capital to Amarna to undermine the ambitions of the priesthood, while Thutmose III reduced their rights and privileges.

In the final years of the Twentieth Dynasty and after conflicts with pharaohs including Ramses XI (1107–1077 BCE), the Amun priesthood had established its own semi-autonomous state in the Thebes region.

SO YOUNG, SO REMEMBERED

Although most people today associate him with the craze of twentieth century CE Egyptomania, Tutankhamun (1341–1323 BCE) only reigned for nine years and did not match the achievements of other pharaohs. However, by the time he died in puzzling circumstances at age 18, he was undefeated in battle, had restored several polytheistic cults and was revered by the public as a deity. On the other hand, his administration had to cope with political turmoil largely caused by his father Akhenaten's sweeping religious reforms.

Tutankhamun did his best to bring cohesion to the realm, reverting Egypt to its traditional polytheistic ways and permitting once again the worship of Amun. Despite being young, Tutankhamun was fortunate to have wise counsellors, including Ay and Horemheb, who likely influenced the significant decisions the boy-pharaoh had to take.

If his life and work lacked glory and success, the discovery of his riches-laden tomb by British archaeologist Howard Carter in 1922 CE (see pages 106–107) has, more than any other event, shaped our modern understanding and appreciation of Ancient Egypt.

DIFFERENT KINDS OF GREAT

Ramses II, nicknamed Ramses the Great (1303–1213 BCE), ruled for 66 years during the Nineteenth Dynasty, lived to around 90, and took Egypt to the zenith of its power and wealth. He was also a great military leader, routing the Hittite Empire at the Battle of Kadesh (see page 34) and turning Egypt into a pre-eminent empire of the time.

Ramses also embarked on a large-scale building programme, commissioning the Ramesseum (his own mortuary temple) in Thebes and the Abu Simbel temples, now a UNESCO World Heritage Site, in Nubia. Something of an egotist, he ordered numerous large statues of himself to be constructed.

THE FECUND PHARAOH

Ramses wasn't short of energy, as he reputedly had over 200 wives and concubines, including some of his daughters. These relationships produced over 100 children, many of whom died before he did. He also suffered from severe arthritis, but it isn't clear if this is connected to the above activities.

HISTORY'S BIGGEST STALEMATE

The Battle of Kadesh (1274 BCE) remains the best-known military confrontation of the pre-Roman ancient world. It is also believed to have involved more chariots (5,000–6,000) than any other battle in history.

Ramses II led about 20,000 men to attack a Hittite army under King Muwatalli II near the city of Kadesh (in present-day Syria). The battle did not begin well for the Egyptians, as they had underestimated the size of the opposing force and were surprised by the Hittites, who had embedded themselves along the Orontes River. For a while, Ramses' men were surrounded and a massacre was on the cards – the pharaoh himself was almost killed – but reinforcements from Egypt prevented this. The battle ended inconclusively, neither side victorious.

Even so, the battle had propaganda uses for Ramses II, helping him to boost his public image as a soldier-pharaoh. Kadesh was immortalized in carvings on the walls of religious buildings, especially the Ramesseum and Karnak, which greatly helped future historians to learn more about the event. The Battle of Kadesh is also remembered for producing arguably the world's first peace treaty, signed between Ramses and Muwatalli.

THE MODERNIZING TRADITIONALIST

The Ptolemaic dynasty, the last to rule in Egypt, was established by a Macedonian, Ptolemy I Soter (367–283 BCE). He had earned a reputation for military excellence as a general under Alexander the Great, who presided over a vast empire from Greece to north-western India. After Alexander died in 323 BCE, his generals became viceroys of various kingdoms, with Ptolemy taking control of Egypt.

Ptolemy I brought law and order to the chaotic kingdom and moved his capital city to Alexandria, which he then developed into a pre-eminent seat of learning and culture. He oversaw the construction of the Heptastadion, an immense causeway, and encouraged trade between European, Arabian and Indian merchants.

Known as a smooth political operator, Ptolemy I styled himself as the natural heir to Egypt's pharaonic customs and as a modernizer open to Greek influence.

FAMILY TIES

Ptolemy I may have been an illegitimate son of Philip II of Macedon, which would have made him Alexander's half-brother.

THE FATHER OF HISTORY

Manetho was a clergyman and arguably the world's first serious historian, who lived during the Ptolemaic era. His magnum opus *Aegyptiaca* (History of Egypt) charts the evolution of Ancient Egypt from its uncertain origins up to his own time. Penned in Greek, it was likely composed during the reign of Ptolemy I, Ptolemy II or Ptolemy III, and its division of Egyptian history into 30 dynasties has strongly influenced our modern framework for understanding the major personalities and events of the civilization.

We are aware of only parts of Manetho's work from allusions to it in the writings of later figures such as the Jewish historian Josephus (37–100 CE) and the Greek bishop Eusebius (260–339 CE). A scholar of many talents, Manetho also explored subjects as diverse as physics, religion, the Greek geographer Herodotus (484–425 BCE) and the correct preparation of *kyphi* (a type of incense). He was also speculated to have been a priest of the sun god Ra, based in the city of Heliopolis.

DECODING THE STONE

Containing a proclamation by King Ptolemy V in 196 BCE explaining his actions and policies to secure the loyalty of the Egyptian people, the Rosetta Stone, a stele made of granodiorite, was crucial to unlocking knowledge about Ancient Egypt. It was discovered in the Egyptian town of Rosetta in 1799 CE by a French soldier serving under Napoleon (see page 132) and later analyzed by Jean-François Champollion and other scholars, who were able to decipher its hieroglyphic and demotic (Egyptian script) inscriptions from the Greek text also on the stone.

The Rosetta Stone fell into British hands in 1801 after the French general Jean-François Menou surrendered to General John Hely-Hutchinson. Regarded as perhaps the most famous Egyptian relic, the stone is now housed in the British Museum. There have been more recent efforts to repatriate the Rosetta Stone to its land of origin, prompting the prominent Egyptologist John Ray to quip, "The day may come when the stone has spent longer in the British Museum than it ever did in Rosetta."

CLEOPATRA AND THE FALL OF EGYPT

The embodiment of female aspiration in Ancient Egypt, Cleopatra VII (69–30 BCE) was the last pharaoh and remains iconic today, having been depicted in film, theatre and literature (see pages 120–4). A gifted and charismatic student, she mastered several languages and the art of political intrigue.

She co-ruled Egypt from 51 BCE with her brother Ptolemy XIII, before relations broke down due to political rivalries and the pressures of fighting both a civil war and a conflict with the Roman Empire. Using her considerable guile and intelligence, Cleopatra wrested power from her brother and became the sole ruler of Egypt.

Cleopatra visited Rome in 48 BCE and started a love affair with Julius Caesar while he was struggling to seize control of Rome. After Caesar was assassinated by his own senators in 44 BCE, Cleopatra formed a romantic and political relationship with Mark Antony in his campaign against Octavian (later Emperor Augustus) to succeed Caesar as Roman emperor.

In 31 BCE, forces commanded by Antony and Cleopatra were defeated by Octavian's navy at the Battle of Actium in the Ionian Sea. Realizing that their bid to

become the power couple of a united Roman-Egyptian state was over, the couple fled to Egypt. Tragically, they both died by suicide in 30 BCE. What exactly happened is still debated, but it appears that Mark Antony stabbed himself with his own sword, believing that Cleopatra had done the same. He survived long enough to be taken to her where he died in her arms. After conducting his burial rites, Cleopatra either drank poison or applied a toxic ointment to her skin.

The Ptolemaic dynasty – and Ancient Egypt as we define it today – was over and now Egypt was a colony of Rome. The Romans tolerated some Egyptian traditions, including mummification and the worship of local deities, but banned some rituals and closed certain temples. Greek-origin Egyptians were given more privileges than the natives and a Roman-appointed governor ruled the new province autocratically.

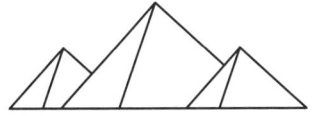

EVERYDAY LIFE

How did an Ancient Egyptian grow up, get educated, marry, work, raise a family and die? What did they eat and drink and do to pass the time? What did they believe in and care about? What was it like to be a woman, a slave, a farmer, a scribe, an artisan or a pharaoh?

Read on to be reassured by the familiar and surprised by the unfamiliar, as while some things change drastically over millennia, others stay constant. By the end of this chapter you might be asking yourself, "Would I like to have spent a day in the life of an Ancient Egyptian?"

THE DELTA DIET

The abundant Nile region supported a balanced diet for most Ancient Egyptians. Bread made from barley and emmer wheat and beer brewed from barley were staples. Wine was preferred by the nobility, with red, white and possibly rosé available.

Ancient Egyptians loved figs, dates, grapes and pomegranates, and used honey as a sweetener. Garlic, onions, leeks, beans and lentils were eaten raw, or in stews cooked in olive oil and spiced with coriander, cumin and dill. Better-off Egyptians ate meat: beef, lamb, mutton and goat meat were consumed alongside *perehen* (duck), *gengen* (goose) and chicken. Fermented cheese and fish were delicacies in some regions. Records show that *iti* (tilapia) from the Nile was the favoured fish, others being *shebti* (catfish) and *bulti* (mullet).

COULD YOU STOMACH THIS?

Poorer people ate fried locusts as a source of protein. Crocodile and hippopotamus were scoffed by the elite class at banquets. Hippo meat has been likened to beef in texture, if fattier and with more fishy and gamy flavours.

PHARAONIC FASHION

Though fashions varied between social groups, breathable linen was the main fabric used in clothing. Women wore long linen gowns held up with shoulder straps. Men donned a linen loincloth and belt. Wealthier men favoured short tunics or robes and, for formal events, mantles draped over the shoulder. Leather or papyrus sandals had unisex appeal.

Pharaohs and elite officials wore variations on the above along with decorative elements, headdresses and crowns. Egyptian men and women alike pioneered make-up, using *kohl* (a dark preparation containing ground-up minerals) as eyeliner, which they believed protected them from the sun's glare.

JEWELS OF THE NILE

Upper-class women accessorized their clothes with jewellery and beads, while richer men displayed jewels on collars or bracelets. Amulets were worn for divine protection. Pharaohs and nobles were often buried with jewellery. Gold, turquoise and lapis lazuli were choice materials, showing off Egyptian craftsmanship.

LONG AS YOU'VE GOT YOUR HEALTH

The discovery of the Ebers and Kahun papyri in the nineteenth century CE proved that the Egyptians knew the human organs and made breakthroughs in dentistry, ophthalmology, dermatology, bone-setting and other forms of surgery. Gynaecology was a distinct discipline that pioneered assisted childbirth, midwifery and uterine surgery. One pregnancy test involved urinating onto barley and emmer wheat – modern science has proven that certain hormones can affect the growth of these plants. The Egyptians saw physical and spiritual well-being as inextricably linked.

MEDICAL ECCENTRICITIES

Modern medicine hasn't vindicated every aspect of Egyptian practices. Magical amulets are no longer thought to protect from illness. When men urinate or defecate blood today it's more likely a symptom of a disease rather than proof that men menstruate too, as the Egyptians believed. Crocodile faeces in one's vagina is not an effective contraceptive. Baldness can't be cured by cooking a greyhound's leg with a donkey's hoof. But no civilization got everything right.

THE CLASS PYRAMID

At the top of the Egyptian social pyramid was the pharaoh, whose supremacy was godly. He or she held supreme executive power and was ultimately responsible for the governance of the state and of the religion.

Next in the pecking order was the vizier, a kind of prime minister to the pharaoh. They were charged with raising taxes, dispensing justice, managing the military and performing other major functions of the state. They were assisted in their duties by a noble class of high priests, generals, politicians and civil servants.

Scribes and artisans constituted the middle class and were highly respected for their skills. They were the intellectual and creative class, drawing up contracts, maintaining records and constructing artefacts and buildings.

Most Egyptians were farmers and unskilled labourers, who grew the crops that fed the civilization and built the pyramids and other large edifices. The lowest of the low were slaves who could never leave their employment on estates or in plush homes unless they were sold on to a new owner. Even so, they had certain rights, including the ability to own property.

STICKING IT TO THE PATRIARCHY

One of the unique traits of Egypt is that, compared to other ancient civilizations, women enjoyed more rights and freedoms. Although, generally, society was male-dominated and most women – especially paupers and slaves – were expected to be dutiful wives, bear children, run households and be subservient to their husbands, they could also run businesses, own property, inherit wealth, make wills, choose their heirs and represent themselves in court.

They could rise up through the ranks of any profession, as demonstrated by female pharaohs such as Hatshepsut, Cleopatra, Neferusobek and Arsinoe. Upper-class women could reach the top of the priesthood to administrate temples and conduct religious services.

Another way in which Egypt was ahead of its time was that a woman had the right to divorce. She could retain her property after marriage and even manage her husband's estate if he died. She was also legally granted custody of her children in the event of a separation.

SLAVERY, BUT NOT AS WE KNOW IT

Slaves were normally prisoners of war or individuals born into slavery. They belonged to one of three categories. Chattel slaves were bought and sold like commodities, a trade that was regulated by the government. Bonded slaves were those who sold themselves into servitude to pay off their debts or get access to food and shelter. Corvée labourers had it slightly easier, as they were compelled to work for a fixed term only.

Slaves could variously be tasked with mining, agriculture, making bricks for construction projects, delivering messages, running errands and performing low-level managerial tasks on estates. Less pleasantly, there were also sex slaves who served as concubines in royal or wealthy households.

Though socially the lowest of the low, slaves in Ancient Egypt had legal rights. They could marry, own property and buy their freedom. The state protected them from abuse, and slavery was not based on racial or ethnic identity, as would be the case in future forms of bondage.

THE WORLD OF WORK

Ancient Egypt had a broad spectrum of needs that had to be catered for by numerous professions. Most people worked in agriculture, since this was essential to the civilization's survival. But, almost as important were skilled masons, potters, carpenters, weavers and jewellers. The goods they made were needed for the maintenance and decoration of the royal court and temples. There would have been no great edifices such as the pyramids without the intellectual labour of engineers and architects.

Priests oversaw religious rites and activities, while soldiers defended the kingdom and were the backbone of Egypt's imperial expansion. Merchants facilitated commerce inside and outside the realm.

IT'S A DIRTY JOB...

Obsessed with grooming, the pharaohs employed personal toenail clippers. There were also designated professional lice removers. Strangest of all to our modern sensibilities, perhaps, were professional mourners who were women hired to weep, rip up their clothes and smother themselves with mud at funerals.

LIVING BY YOUR PEN

Scribes were educated in special schools and had a deep understanding of the written languages of the time. Employed by the pharaonic state, the temples and the royal court, they were the lifeblood of officialdom, responsible for keeping records of taxation, trade, land ownership and the census. They also recorded legal cases and wrote contracts, and were responsible for copying hymns, funerary texts, religious narratives, fictional stories, and guides to etiquette and manners.

Excused from manual labour and enjoying more privileges than the average citizen, scribes were tasked with preserving Egyptian civilization. They tended to write on papyri using reed brushes or carve inscriptions into stone, and much of our modern understanding of Ancient Egypt comes from their efforts.

The Satire of the Trades, emerging at the time of the Middle Kingdom, gave scribes their due by praising their important work while simultaneously lampooning other professions. Preserved on a papyrus, this text is now in the Louvre Museum in Paris.

STATE OF THE ART AND CRAFT

Seen at the time as almost as important to Egyptian culture as scribes, the artisan class produced the artwork and other items required by palaces, temples, tombs and ordinary homes. Each artisan had a specialism, such as weaving, woodworking, metalworking, stone carving, pottery and jewellery making.

If architects and engineers designed the pyramids, it was the artisans who were responsible for producing the elaborate statues, reliefs and inscriptions that commemorated gods and pharaohs. Some artisans were recruited for big-scale projects by pharaohs and high-level officials, while others were self-employed, making goods for daily use and trade.

DOWNING TOOLS

The first recorded successful strike in history was in 1157 BCE when Egyptian artisans refused to carry on working for Pharaoh Ramses III (1186–1155 BCE) when there was a delay in paying their wages, which came mainly in the form of beer and grain. They occupied temples until they received what was owed to them.

HARSH LESSONS

Although Ancient Egypt made several important steps forward in gender equality (see page 46), education was definitely skewed in favour of boys, who were sent to school, whereas girls were taught domestic skills in the home. Class played a role too, with higher-born boys more likely to receive schooling in preparation for careers in scribing, the priesthood or politics.

Literacy was paramount, with children learning hieroglyphics and, later on, hieratic and demotic scripts. Specialist scribe schools were usually sited near temples or government buildings. In addition, young Egyptians learned grammar, mathematics, citizenship, morality and theology.

Teachers were often veteran scribes who gave their students key texts to copy and inscribe. They would practise on *ostraca* (fragments of broken pottery) or limestone flakes. Accounting and record-keeping were also taught, as were spells that were thought to have healing and protective effects.

If you misbehaved in class you could expect a zero-tolerance reaction. A popular phrase of the time was "The ear of a boy is on his back; he listens when he is beaten."

EVERYONE KNOWS THEIR PLACE

Ancient Egypt was as far from a democracy as we would understand it today, its political structure extremely centralized and hierarchical, with the pharaoh the unquestioned and divine ruler. As the gods' envoy, the pharaoh had full power over the kingdom, its people and its resources. The pharaoh had a broad portfolio, at once a spiritual leader responsible for ensuring *maat* (order and justice), the supreme military commander and the overseer of the building of monuments and significant buildings.

Beneath the pharaoh was a tight-knit system of bureaucrats and executives. The vizier's job was to implement the pharaoh's wishes regarding governance, law and taxation. Other important senior managers were nomarchs who ran *nomes* (Egypt's provinces). There were also senior clerics, particularly those belonging to the priesthood of Amun (see page 31), generals and ministers in charge of trade and construction.

There was a revolving door between the priestly caste and politics, with numerous figures holding positions in both systems. High priests managed the major temples.

GOOD AND BAD ADVICE

Ancient Egyptian notions of modesty, fairness, decency and compassion were shaped by the *Instruction of Ptahhotep*, a guide to moral virtue and efficient governance penned by the vizier Ptahhotep, who lived and worked sometime during the Fifth Dynasty of the Old Kingdom.

The text comprises advice for a young man beginning his adult life and career, inculcating in him the importance of honesty, incorruptibility and the pursuit of harmony. Its teachings were designed to improve citizenship, warning against the perils of talking too much and coming under the influence of foolish people. Ptahhotep cautions against arguing with such fools, for this is a waste of time.

Ptahhotep is credited with bolstering Ancient Egypt's image as a civilization that valued intellectual endeavour, as he suggests that writing and scholarship will ensure that a person is always remembered and respected. He also advises young men to avoid the desires of women who might lead them astray. Old age is dismissed as a nasty stage of life in which "The mouth is silent, speech fails him; the mind decays, remembering not the day before."

THE FATHER OF AFRICAN RIVERS

The Nile River had an extraordinary impact on almost every aspect of everyday Egyptian life. It is doubtful whether the civilization would ever have started without it, given the river's essential role in agriculture, travel and trade.

The Nile's yearly floods provided nutrient-abundant silt to the land, supporting the growth of crops essential to survival – from wheat to flax and barley, and a panoply of vegetables. The Nile irrigated the drier regions of inland Egypt, allowing for the expansion of the population and the establishment of new towns and cities. A range of fish and waterfowl were available in the river, and its water was used by those who dwelled around it for drinking, cooking and washing.

The bonanzas brought by new trade networks with the Levant and Nubia would have been impossible without the Nile allowing the import and export of food, luxury commodities and raw materials by boat and raft. The Nile's role as a natural highway also promoted the cultural interactions that helped Egypt thrive and evolve, such as those with Ancient Greece during the Ptolemaic dynasty.

The river also allowed the smooth and rapid deployment of soldiers for Egypt's foreign military interventions and served as a supply line. The Nile's cataracts (rapids) formed a natural defence against invading Kushites and Nubians.

Egyptians revered the Nile as a signifier of the pharaoh's divine power and as a holy site in its own right, inextricably tied to Hapi, the deity representing the annual floods, known in spiritual terms as the *Akhet* (the Inundation). The floods were thought to be the tears of Isis as she mourned her husband, Osiris, the god of fertility. According to legend, Osiris' remains were scattered in the Nile by his brother Set.

PLANT POWER

The all-important papyrus plant grew all over the banks of the Nile. A symbol of wealth and vitality in Egyptian culture, it was used to make boats, baskets, mats, clothes and shoes. Perhaps most crucially to the civilization's development, papyrus was used to make the paper on which records were kept, contracts were made and decrees issued.

KEEPING IT CLEAN

Ahead of their time in yet another way, Ancient Egyptians were fixated on personal hygiene and cleanliness, regarding it as essential to both physical and spiritual health. They bathed daily, often in the waters of the Nile. The rich were assisted by their servants in washing, while ordinary citizens used clay, animal fat or natron (a natural salt) as a cleansing agent.

Egyptians kept their mouths and teeth clean by chewing on twigs from aromatic trees. Toothpaste was made from ashes, pumice and crushed eggshells. All of this was probably necessitated by the Egyptian diet of sand-contaminated grain and thick bread, which damaged teeth.

Head-shaving was common to prevent lice, as was wearing wigs made from human hair or plants (see page 102). There is evidence that Egyptians wore perfumed wax cones on top of their heads to distribute fragrance over a long period. Priests often shaved all the hair on their bodies in the belief that it would bring them closer to the gods.

ABODES FIT FOR PHARAOHS AND OTHERS

Most lower- and middle-class Egyptians dwelled in unbaked mud-brick homes with flat roofs made from clay or palm fronds. In the warmer months, the family would gather on these roofs to relax in the evening or to sleep at night. Such houses were based around a central yard and often had lounges, kitchens and bedrooms, a garden and a well. Walls were decorated with paintings of day-to-day life and the homes of better-off individuals had ornately crafted furniture. Windows were uncommon, as Egyptians got more than enough sun when out and about.

Pharaohs and other elite personages lived in royal estates such as the Great Palace of Akhetaten and the Malkata Palace in Thebes. On the premises were farms, artisanal workshops, private gardens, artificial lakes, granaries, servants' quarters and monumental buildings such as a *per-aa* (grand palace) replete with large courtyards, halls and chambers. A primitive form of air-conditioning was made possible in rooms by airflow spaces made in the walls. Furniture was made from ebony and ivory, and beds were often perfumed and sometimes inlaid with gold and even lion's paws.

KEEPING ORDER

The legal system was rooted in the principles of *maat*. Upholding the law was synonymous with ensuring harmony, balance and the pre-eminence of the pharaoh in society. Their decisions in matters of law and order were final.

However, a complex and advanced court system meant that others had a say in verdicts too. Trials and hearings were presided over by a judge, with citizens representing themselves or using advocates. Appeals and serious misdemeanours were often heard by the pharaoh themself.

We know from papyri and tomb carvings about Egyptian laws pertaining to marriage, trade, inheritance and property rights. Punishments for minor crimes ranged from written warnings to fines, while corruption and theft could earn you a public flogging.

WOULD YOU BE DETERRED BY THIS?

If you committed murder or treason, or robbed or desecrated a tomb, you could end up with the death penalty. Beheading was the most common method, followed by burning alive, drowning in the Nile and being impaled on a stake.

GETTING THROUGH THE DAY

In Ancient Egypt, if you were sick, plagued by money worries, needed to pass an exam, wanted someone to fall in love with you or had any other common human needs or wants, then you would visit a temple and participate in the daily rites designed to curry favour with the gods, and leave offerings of food, incense and treasure at the statues of these deities. You might also stay home and involve yourself in smaller, more intimate ceremonies. Egyptians paid homage to the sun god Ra each morning, praying that the day would turn out well for them.

Many professions were directly connected to religion, with priests, artisans and scribes looking after temples and recording holy texts. Farmers made tributes to the gods to ensure good harvests.

Major public festivals, such as Opet in Thebes, would involve sacrifices, banquets and processions that would display statues and effigies of the gods on barges.

Religious devotion was also a private matter, with every Egyptian from every walk of life trying to live according to the diktats of *maat*, showing humility, patience, respect and honesty at all times.

THE MUMMY STATE

Utterly unique to Ancient Egypt, mummies and their burial processes have been an invaluable font of knowledge about this great civilization. After an Egyptian died, their soul could only survive in the afterlife if their body was preserved through an arduous process called mummification. The process took over two months and began with the extraction of the lungs, liver, stomach and intestines through an incision in the abdomen, as these were the body parts that deteriorated the quickest. The heart was not removed, as it was believed to contain the soul and to be the centre of thought and intelligence. The brain, on the other hand, was often sucked or hooked out through the corpse's nostrils.

The body was then coated with natron, which dehydrated the flesh and prevented decomposition. The evidence suggests this process took 40 days.

Once the body was dry, the skin was covered with oils and resins to preserve it and give the impression that it was still alive.

At this point the now-iconic linen bandages would be wrapped around the body and amulets embedded between the layers for spiritual protection. The scarab,

representing resurrection, was the most important of these amulets.

The mummified body would then be put into a coffin or an elaborate, multi-section sarcophagus, usually made from wood, granite or limestone. These containers were adorned with images and spells thought to ensure smooth passage to the hereafter. In later Egyptian times, particularly during the New Kingdom, only notable people would have sarcophagi, which were often designed to resemble those buried within them.

Full-scale mummification and burial were typically only for the wealthy and privileged, but as Egyptian civilization evolved and especially after the religious revolutions, the option became available to non-elite Egyptians.

WEIRD TRAVEL COMPANIONS

Grave goods were always placed into coffins alongside mummies. Stranger items included *shabtis*, miniature dolls that would assist the deceased in their journey, and fake food made from clay or wood, which was intended to feed the mummy in the next world. Cats, monkeys, birds and even crocodiles were also mummified and sometimes buried with humans.

SOMETHING TO BELIEVE IN

For most of Ancient Egypt's existence, polytheism was dominant, with a vast pantheon of deities who controlled various facets of existence. There was no escape from religion in daily Egyptian life and everyone, rich or poor, powerful or inconsequential, was expected to maintain the values of *maat* and believe in the cosmic cycle of birth, death and rebirth.

Atum (meaning "the complete one") was thought to be the first deity and was often later merged with Ra, who represented life and creation. Each day, so the belief had it, Ra would travel across the sky and then at night enter the underworld. He would be resurrected the next morning and the process would begin again.

Amun started out as a minor deity of mystery in the locale of Thebes before being promoted to pre-eminence in the reign of Ramses II. In time, Atum and Amun came to be merged in Egyptian religion.

Other major deities included falcon-headed Horus, of whom the pharaoh was the mortal embodiment. Osiris was god of the afterlife and resurrection. Motherly and wifely ideals were represented by his wife, Isis, while his brother Set presided over the chaos and destruction of the natural and supernatural planes.

Lesser gods included the lion-faced Babi (symbolizing strength and violence), Taweret who protected women during childbirth with her crocodile's tail and hippo's head, Khonsu (time and healing), Serqet (funeral rites), the diminutive Bes (domestic life) and Anubis (mummification and the afterlife).

Religion compelled one to not only live well but to die well too. Upon death, Egyptians believed that you travelled through *Duat* (the underworld) to the Hall of Judgement, whereupon your heart was weighed against the Feather of *Maat* as a test of your piety. If you passed, you would be treated to eternal life in *Aaru* (the Field of Reeds). If not, your soul would be devoured by the female demon Ammit and you'd have to spend perpetuity in *Duat*.

STUCK IN THE UNDERWORLD

Duat was not a hell-like place of constant torment as per Abrahamic religions, but somewhere one had to live miserably without a soul or intellect. *Duat*'s geography was depicted as similar to the real world only with the addition of iron walls, fiery lakes and trees made from turquoise.

A SOLDIER'S LIFE

Many Egyptians were conscripted into the military in times of war. The armed forces made many leaps forward in the New Kingdom era when soldiers began to specialize in archery (using flexible and robust composite bows), sword and spear fighting, or chariotry. Egypt pioneered chariot combat, with vehicles usually drawn by donkeys or horses and having the advantage of being speedy and hardy in a combat situation.

Egyptian armies were highly disciplined and hierarchical, commanded at the top level by either the pharaoh or a high-level official who made long- and short-term tactical decisions. Officers directed smaller units. As an employee of the military, you would not just be expected to fight wars of aggression. Sometimes you would be ordered to help defend borders, billeted in one of the sturdy fortresses in the Nile Delta and along key trade routes. Soldiers could also be recruited to help with the building of large edifices such as pyramids.

Like the office of the pharaoh, the military was regarded as a representative and defender of the gods' will.

THE BOTTOM LINE

Ordinary life was hugely enriched by Egypt's role as a major economy, with precious stones, cedar wood and copper flooding into the kingdom as a result of trade with societies in Nubia, the Levant and the Mediterranean region, and, further afield, the Indus Valley and Mesopotamia. Egypt's valuable exports included gold, grain, linen and papyrus, and there was an array of jobs that supported these industries.

Merchants and artisans, among other professions, were taxed by the state in the form of grain. This in turn was allocated to armies, government workers and those working in temples. Craftspeople made jewellery, pottery, furniture and tools, and sold them at bustling markets in cities like Thebes and, later, Memphis and Alexandria. Here, too, would be sold food, spices, clothes and just about anything else a citizen needed. The main currency was, again, grain, but bartering for goods was also common.

Royal and private merchants would provide the rich and powerful with deluxe items such as gold, incense, perfume, papyrus scrolls, exotic pets like gazelles and elephants, and wine from places like Canaan.

LOVE AND MARRIAGE

As with other civilizations throughout history, marriage in Egypt was an institution that cemented family alliances and lineages. Marriages were normally arranged on behalf of younger relatives by senior family members. The bride's father negotiated a dowry, a gift or payment made to the bride's clan, to facilitate the marriage.

Only the well-off had wedding ceremonies, which featured feasts and dances and a public exchange of vows. For most Egyptians, marriage contracts would be drawn up and witnessed by scribes, stipulating mutual responsibilities and expectations, and the happy couple would start living together.

Husbands and wives generally had equal rights within marriage. Adultery was taboo, but it happened.

KEEPING IT IN THE FAMILY

As repulsive as it may seem to us today, incest was common in Egypt. Ancient pharaohs were even expected to marry their own siblings – but uncles, aunts, cousins, nieces, mothers and sons could also become spouses. Tutankhamun bucked the trend slightly – he shacked up with his half-sister.

PROTO-NUCLEAR FAMILIES

More familiar to us, perhaps, is the family structure of Ancient Egypt, which typically consisted of a father, mother and children living under one roof. It was customary for the father to go out to work and the mother to oversee the household and look after the kids, although both parties were expected to uphold *maat* in the home and ensure that the family was respectable and prosperous.

Children were valued and boys given the best education that their families could afford. They were taught to respect their parents and elders, in keeping with Amenemhat the pharaoh's dictum: "Your mother is the one who gave you life, and your heart should be devoted to her. Do not forsake her in her old age."

Families would gather inside the home for meals and for religious rites conducted at household shrines. Families would be responsible for arranging the funerals of their relatives, paying for mummification and grave goods if they could afford them. Another barrier to entering the afterlife was having a poor relationship with your family.

PURIFICATION

In the Ptolemaic Period, public baths emerged in Egypt, influenced by Greek and Roman culture. The bigger baths were in metropolises like Thebes and Alexandria, sited near markets, temples (and sometimes inside them), palaces and other significant places. They were as much to do with relaxation, socialization and religion as hygiene.

Cleanliness was next to godliness for Egyptians, and a visit to the baths was a surefire way to achieve such purification. After the introduction of public baths in Egypt, the gods were believed to require mortals to show their piety by bathing four times a day: in the morning, midday, evening and night-time.

Bathers would plunge themselves into networks of pools or chambers filled with water and wash their sweat and dirt away. Sometimes attendants would scrape visitors clean with curved bronze implements, similar to Ancient Greek *strigils* (a curved tool). They would then apply perfumed oils to their skin. Some public baths included saunas and steam rooms, indicating that the Egyptians knew of the mental and physical health benefits of heat. In public baths people would also chat, share stories and jokes, and strike business deals.

LGBTQ+ EGYPT?

There are no explicit references to sexuality in surviving Ancient Egyptian texts, but there are clues to the existence of same-sex relationships and gender fluidity.

Nyankh-khnum and Khnum-hotep, high-ranking officials of the Fifth Dynasty, were buried in the same *mastaba*, suggesting that they were intimate. Paintings inside the tomb show them hugging one another and touching noses. Some but not all scholars have taken this as evidence that homosexuality was permitted in Ancient Egypt, at least between two men who were married to women and had children, which was true of this duo.

A tomb picture from the Eighteenth Dynasty depicts Senet and Neferu, two royal women, holding hands – a gesture that was customary in romantic unions. However, there is not a consensus among historians about this. It is possible that Pharaoh Ramses II had a gay relationship with a man called Bay, his personal chariot driver. Again, not all scholars who have deciphered the inscriptions and images relating to these men agree on that interpretation.

The female pharaoh Hatshepsut (see page 22) was depicted as having masculine and feminine traits, while several deities have androgynous appearances.

ANIMALS WERE FIRST-CLASS CITIZENS

From our modern perspective, one of the stranger – though in some ways more enlightened – facets of Egyptian culture is the worship of animals, which were often the manifestations of deities and supernatural forces.

Cats were the most revered creatures, associated with the goddess Bastet, who had lion-like features and denoted fertility and protection. You could be sentenced to death for killing a cat, even accidentally. Representing the god Horus, falcons and hawks were ciphers of royal authority, and pharaohs were often depicted with the heads of the former.

Prefiguring Hinduism by some centuries, Egyptians held cows to be sacred, especially the sacred Apis bull of Memphis. They were believed to be the earthly representatives of the deity Ptah. Flamboyant rituals marked the Apis bull's death and burial. The deity Sobek had a crocodile's head and a man's body, and so it makes sense that crocodiles were linked to him, as were hippopotamuses.

The cobra god Wadjet was thought to protect Lower Egypt, and the snake would appear on the pharaoh's crown as a symbol of holy security and supremacy.

On a smaller scale, scarab beetles were worshipped by Egyptians, who held that their ability to roll dung balls reflected the god Khepri's task of pushing the sun over the sky, symbolizing rebirth and transformation. Scarabs were ubiquitous on amulets worn day-to-day and placed in coffins and sarcophagi.

Many temples were dedicated to creatures or animal-headed gods. The relevant animals were kept in the temples and looked after by priests. When they died, they were mummified using the same process as that for humans and buried with full ritual honours, sometimes in large tombs.

POLICE BABOONS

Not only did Egyptians keep pet baboons, but these animals were also trained to pick fruit, dance and do police work. Like today's sniffer dogs, baboons were used to guard properties and to track down and help catch criminals. In paintings from the time, baboons are shown performing policing or legal roles as humans might, which is taken as a metaphor for their involvement in sniffing out miscreants. Baboons were associated with Thoth, the god of insight and reasoning.

ART AND CULTURE

Ancient Egypt's culture was singular and original in multiple ways, as we will see from its innovations in language, literature, architecture, music, dance and sport. But it also borrowed from neighbouring and invading civilizations, adapting its intellectual life, artistic techniques and religious practices to new social circumstances.

The story of Egyptian culture is a rich and intricate one, so be prepared for strange and amusing anecdotes and contradictions that will make you scratch your head... and hopefully want to understand and appreciate it more.

THE FIRST LITERATURE

Few literary traditions are as old as Ancient Egypt's and they offer those of us alive today extraordinary insights into the civilization's customs, principles and attitudes. The earliest known writings originated in the Old Kingdom and are found on rocks, stones, papyri and tomb walls. These are hardly rollicking stories – they provided useful religious, political, administrative and funerary information for people of the time.

The Pyramid Texts of the Fifth and Sixth dynasties are the oldest examples of religious writing on Earth. They were inscribed on pyramid walls and intended to safeguard the pharaohs when they entered the afterlife.

First found on coffins of the Middle Kingdom period, the Coffin Texts focused on dead Egyptians' voyages to the underworld and the process by which they turned into *akhs* (blessed spirits). Spell number 1,000 in the Coffin Texts is intended to "drive away hippopotamuses" – a reference to defending the deceased from molestation by the aggressive goddess Taweret.

The *Book of the Dead* dates to the New Kingdom and was a compilation mostly on papyri of magical incantations, prayers and instructions that became popular with ordinary Egyptians, not just elite ones.

WORDS AS PICTURES

Hieroglyphics was the groundbreaking writing system of Ancient Egypt, famous for its complex use of pictures and symbols. It had an immense influence on almost every element of Egyptian society.

Emerging in the Early Dynastic Period, the word "hieroglyph" means "sacred carving" in reference to their use in religious texts that were carved in wood or stone and found in tombs, on monuments and on temple walls. Amounting to 700 symbols in total, some hieroglyphs alluded to phenomena in the world, while others were logograms and phonograms (both representing sounds), determinatives (clarifying word meanings) and syllables (syllabic signs). This means that hieroglyphics also constituted an alphabetic system.

Unlike modern languages, hieroglyphics could be written in any direction: right to left, left to right or top to bottom. To figure out which way to read them you must look at which direction the human or animal figures are facing. The writers and readers of hieroglyphics loved puns: the symbol *hpr* can mean both "scarab beetle" and the verbs "to become" or "to transform".

Later, hieroglyphics came to be written on papyri with reed pens and ink made from water and soot.

Most Egyptians were not hieroglyphics-literate – only priests, scribes and nobles knew the language.

Hieroglyphics cannot be disentangled from religion, since they were used in the Pyramid Texts, Coffin Texts and *Book of the Dead*. But they were also the language of commemoration and record-keeping. The reigns of pharaohs, great battles and other events were all rendered in hieroglyphics.

Sometimes hieroglyphics could prove controversial. Pharaohs who succeeded Akhenaten tried to suppress knowledge of his religious reforms by having their artisans chisel his name and allusions to his sun god, Aten, out of walls and stones. Similar censorship happened to the legacy of Hatshepsut.

By the close of the Ptolemaic period, hieroglyphics had been superseded by the demotic and Greek scripts. Their influence lived on, though, with the Greeks and Romans using hieroglyphics for temple inscriptions until around 400 CE.

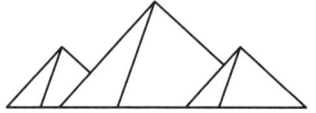

WRITERS ARE SACRED

One of the philosophical beliefs of Ancient Egyptians was that writing was a holy activity and that scribes and wordsmiths would enjoy safe passage to the afterlife. The short text *The Immortality of Writers*, likely used to teach Egyptian children and attributed to a man called Irsesh who lived during the Nineteenth or Twentieth dynasties, claims: "Man perishes; his corpse turns to dust; all his relatives return to the earth. But writings make him remembered in the mouth of the reader. A book is more effective than a well-built house or a tomb-chapel, better than an established villa or a stela in the temple!"

When commissioned to compose tomb inscriptions, scribes would include in them prayers for their own immortality, requesting to the gods that their work be remembered and cherished for eternity. In the earthly realm, too, one's skill at writing was seen as a way of guaranteeing one's legacy and influence on future generations.

The Immortality of Writers is recorded on a papyrus and now held in the British Museum.

PYRAMID AESTHETICS

The design and look of the pyramids remains impressive to us, some 4,000 years after their construction. Their inimitable shape was not chosen randomly; it was a cipher for the benben stone, the first land that emerged after the retreat of *Nun* (the Waters of Chaos), according to the Ancient Egyptian creation myth.

The sloping sides of pyramids were believed to help the deceased pharaoh rise to the heavens. Precise calculations were required to ensure that these sides were horizontally and vertically balanced. The angles of the Pyramid of Giza are 51.5 degrees, so that the sides reflect the sun effectively, which speaks to Ancient Egyptian reverence for the solar disc and proves that the Egyptians had advanced knowledge of astronomy. Giza was also painstakingly aligned with the four compass points.

The first pyramids shone like divine beacons, linking the natural and supernatural planes, thanks to their smooth texture, achieved by the use of polished limestone.

The Red Pyramid, built in the Fourth Dynasty, is regarded as the inaugural "true pyramid" due to its

smooth, even slope. Its proportions are balanced and thus in keeping with the ethos of *maat*. The pyramid's reddish colour is a function of the type of limestone used. Few buildings are as visually beguiling as this.

The beauty of the paintings and objets d'art inside the pyramids was matched by the design of their interior rooms, with meticulously planned corridors, burial chambers, air shafts that lined up with certain stars, and the application of corbelling, a method by which layers of stone overlap one another.

AN ARRESTING ACCIDENT

The Bent Pyramid (*c.* 2600 BCE) is not just a clever name. It has a steep angle at its bottom, which turns into a low slope near its top. It is speculated that this singular shape, now famous, came out of an effort to rectify structural weaknesses that were noticed during an earlier construction phase.

THE PHASES OF EGYPTIAN ART

Like other grand civilizations, Egypt underwent an evolution in its artistic styles and approaches. In the Predynastic Period, art focused on funerary and spiritual motifs, with pottery and figurines crafted into geometric shapes dominating. Unfussy but richly symbolic artefacts like vases and carvings emerged in this phase.

The Old Kingdom saw the construction of the first pyramids, and large-scale sculptures and tomb art that offered vivid if highly stylized portrayals of the pharaohs and other personages.

During the Middle Kingdom, the arts and crafts diversified and verisimilitude came to the fore with efforts made to realistically represent well-known people and scenes of everyday life and, indeed, the afterlife.

The proud and powerful New Kingdom brought stunning tomb paintings, grandiose temples and colossal statues. The expansion of the Egyptian empire meant that artists were inspired by new ideas, figures and locations. In addition to pharaohs and gods, foreign lands became the subjects of pictures. There was an even greater emphasis on naturalism during the reign

of Akhenaten, with more literal portrayals of the royal family now in vogue.

In the final centuries of Ancient Egypt, when the civilization was absorbing Greek and Persian cultural forms, artefacts became more ornate and detailed, with techniques such as cartonnage (the coating of linen or papyrus with plaster) applied to coffins, and the inclusion of gold, lapis lazuli and faience (a glazed ceramic) in jewellery and figurines. Progress in glass-making was seen in the Ptolemaic period, with gorgeous beads and vessels produced. At this time, though, there was a revival of previous Egyptian forms, with statues in rigid, determined poses harking back to the glory days of pharaonic divinity.

INTRIGUING SCENES

Nebamun was an elite official in the Eighteenth Dynasty, whose tomb is acclaimed for its dynamic colours and recreations of meaningful events in his life. In one frieze, wild beasts jump around Nebamun while he is on a hunting expedition in swamplands. In others he is seen trying to spear birds from a boat and banqueting with his family, the pet cat prowling around.

SOME ANIMALS WERE LESS EQUAL

The Egyptians worshipped some creatures and killed others for food and entertainment. Egyptian commoners hunted primarily to eat and expeditions could involve a family travelling out into the Nile by boat and throwing sticks at birds to stun them. Bows and lassos were also popular weapons.

For the noble class, hunting was a sport and a means of showing off one's prestige and power. The Nile region was abundant with wildfowl, antelopes, gazelles, deer and wild boar. The more daring party might risk pursuing lions and hippopotamuses, which were difficult to kill. However, success in these enterprises demonstrated a pharaoh's or nobleman's courage and bravery, thereby having political and reputational advantages. As defender and ruler of the land, it was important for the pharaoh to prove that they could subdue any creature on that land.

In the early days of the kingdom, hunters would go out into the desert on foot. Later they preferred chariots for their speed and manoeuvrability, especially if they were tracking big game that might suddenly charge at them.

DEEP AND MEANINGFUL SONGS

Historians cannot always be sure whether Ancient Egyptian texts were intended to be recited or sung. What have come to be called *Harper's Songs*, originating in the Middle Kingdom period, are thought to have belonged to the latter category because the original inscriptions were accompanied by striking pictures of blind harpists.

The songs tell us much about the Egyptian worldview, laying the groundwork for future philosophies of rationalism and scepticism by advising people to savour life since it is an experience that is fleeting and transitory. Potentially controversial for the time, the text known as "Harper's Song from the Tomb of King Intef" comes close to questioning the existence of the afterlife and emphasizing making the most of the mortal life. Other songs ruminate on death, love, longing, desire and happiness.

"The Dispute Between a Man and His Ba" is presented as an argument between a man and his soul. The text comments on the pain and suffering of the earthly world, speculates on what death might be like and considers its capacity to be a levelling force given that all humans, rich or poor, must die.

PASSING THE TIME

Ancient Egyptians loved to unwind with sports and games, these often also sharpening military skills and increasing religious knowledge. We know from tomb art and objects that perhaps the most popular board game was *Senet*, played on a rectangular grid. The objective was to be the first player to shift all their pieces off the board. Senet was thought to be a metaphor for the transition of the soul to the next world.

Our modern-day Snakes and Ladders almost certainly owes something to *Mehen*, given that the aim of this game was to move pieces along a serpent-shaped board. The winner was the first to reach the head of the beast.

Checkers is thought to have evolved from the Egyptian Hounds and Jackals, a strategy game won by trapping your adversary's pieces. This too was deemed to represent the great trip to the hereafter. The oddity about Hounds and Jackals is that it may not have had fixed rules and that magic was thought to be involved in its playing.

Less sedentary pastimes included rowboat racing on the Nile, gymnastics, wrestling and boxing, about which we know from surviving works of art. If you were any good at javelin throwing, archery or running, you might

go on to a glittering career in the pharaoh's army.

Archery contests were popular and used live birds and small mammals as targets – something of a challenge. Pharaoh Ramses II won many of these competitions and this complemented his military victories. Pharaoh Amenemhat (1939–1910 BCE) was also a keen and accomplished archer from what we can glean from tomb reliefs. We have reason to believe that sporting competitions formed part of the flamboyant ceremonies during which pharaohs were coronated.

Also familiar to the sportspeople of today is tug of war, in which teams of Egyptians would stand either side of a line or a pit and compete to pull a rope. The all-purpose material papyrus has been found inside multicoloured leather balls that were used in an Ancient Egyptian precursor to our field hockey. The sticks were palm tree branches. It also appears that Egyptians played a version of our contemporary handball.

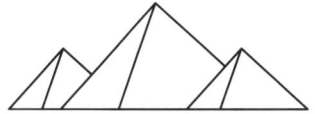

PROTO-THEATRE

Modern drama owes much to the conventions of Ancient Greek and Roman plays. However, Ancient Egyptian theatre was something quite different. Dramatic performances were intimately bound with holy rituals and festivals, and involved music, dance, singing and incantations. The plots of these performances were, unsurprisingly, faithful to the biographies of various deities.

The *Passion Play*, dating back at least to the Middle Kingdom, was an integral part of the Opet Festival in Thebes. It was a take on the story of the goddess Isis' quest to find the body of her husband, Osiris, and was staged in temples. Its performers wore elaborate costumes and would make flamboyant gestures to mirror the gods' power and authority.

GODS PULLING THE STRINGS

During the Middle and Late kingdoms, Egypt made several advances in puppetry: wood or clay dolls had moving parts; shadow puppets were made of linen and "Osirian figures" were movable figurines. It was believed that dead ancestors and the pantheon of gods could be summoned through such performances.

POTTERY

Having both functional and spiritual value, Ancient Egyptian pottery was primarily made of clay from the Nile River's banks. Artisans would form this clay either by hand or with a potter's wheel, a method that probably originated during the New Kingdom.

Egyptian pottery is remarkable for its flat and shiny texture and decoration with striking geometric figures or symbols referencing deities and sacred animals. Exquisite funerary pots would be left inside tombs filled with food to provide the deceased with sustenance in the hereafter.

A unique aspect of Egyptian ceramics was the production of scale models portraying ordinary life. These would include human figures and minute boats and chariots and would also be placed in tombs to assist with the epic trip to the afterlife.

DRIVEN BY DUNG

Some artisans would reinforce their Nile silt or marl (limestone) clay with animal droppings, while donkey dung was used to fuel the kilns in some workshops. How this must have smelled – especially to a society that valued cleanliness – we don't know.

MAKING A SONG AND DANCE

As with theatre, Ancient Egyptian music and dance were inseparable from holy ritual, not least because these art forms were thought to summon the divine into everyday life. Music and dance were present at funerals but were also popular forms of entertainment, enjoyed at celebrations of military victories, coronations, jubilees and public feasts. Buskers would perform in markets and public squares.

The lute, harp and lyre were ubiquitous stringed instruments, while wind instruments ranged from flutes to double-reed pipes. Drums and cymbals brought a due sense of bombast and ordered rhythm to proceedings. The sistrum was a singular Egyptian invention, taking the form of a horseshoe-shaped handheld instrument made from copper, bronze and/or wood. The sistrum was understood to secure the favour of the goddess Hathor, whose purview, unsurprisingly, included music and dance.

Dancing was a unisex activity, common at the events mentioned above, and synchronized with musical performances. Dance moves were poised and graceful and tended to signify themes such as fertility and harvest.

Dancing was also a professionalized discipline, with people apprenticed at a young age to troupes that would be hired to perform in temples or at the pharaonic court.

We know from tomb reliefs that, in the Old Kingdom, there was a specialized troupe of female dancers called the Acacia House. They performed at funerary rites after the mummification process was complete, with the objective of appropriately mourning the dead and pleasing the goddess Sekhmet.

Surviving across all the kingdoms was the *mww*, another holy ensemble of dancers, who wore skirts and cone-shaped headdresses of reed or palm fibre that denoted their role as ferrymen/women. Their performance symbolically sent the dead person down to the underworld.

During the Middle and New Kingdom epochs, a Hathor-dedicated dance was particularly energetic, with performers jumping and skipping to booming drum beats, clapping and stick-hitting. A sung or spoken incantation would accompany the din.

SOUL-CLUED

The Ancient Egyptian conception of the human soul was highly sophisticated for its time. The soul was comprised of constituent elements, each having a specific purpose. The parts, nonetheless, had to work together in harmony and balance to guarantee a good life and, more importantly, a good afterlife.

Ka was a fundamental life force, conceptualized as the spiritual double of an individual. It was thought to reside in the body during a person's mortal lifetime and could take leave of that body after death. The food left inside tombs was believed to nourish *ka*.

A human's personality was intimately bound up with the notion of *ba*. Upon death, *ba* could transition between the natural and supernatural worlds, but it ultimately had to settle in the body for its spirit to rest in peace.

Ib was associated with the heart, and thus the axis of human morality and compassion. Your *ib* had to be in good shape if you were going to be judged favourably in the underworld. *Akh* was the immortal substance of an Egyptian, supposing they had successfully arrived in the afterlife.

SMALL BUT DIVINELY FORMED

Another of Ancient Egypt's idiosyncrasies is that pygmies and dwarves were regarded as having supernatural powers, particularly in the Early Dynastic and Old Kingdom eras. Linked to the diminutive deity Bes, the guardian of women, children and the domestic sphere, people of short stature were thought to have a celestial knack for healing, craftsmanship, protecting women during childbirth and warding off evil.

The First Dynasty saw people with dwarfism employed directly by the pharaoh's court. When they died they were given the honour of being buried in tombs near those of their masters. In the Old Kingdom, they found gainful work as dancers, jewellers, gardeners and tailors.

By the time of the New Kingdom, prejudice had come to taint Egyptian attitudes to people with dwarfism and pygmies. The papyrus entitled *The Wise Doctrine of Amenemope, Son of Kanakht* mentions incidents of abuse and calls for the fairer treatment of the community.

We know about attitudes to dwarfism in Ancient Egypt thanks to the relatively naturalistic portrayal of people in objets d'art and the fact that no fewer than three words were used to signify them.

FESTIVAL TIME

While festivals were taken seriously as gateways to the divine, securing the goodwill of the gods towards everything from personal aspiration to the next harvest, they were also joyful, noisy and vibrant events.

The new agricultural season would be ushered in by the *Wepet Renpet* (Festival of the New Year). The annual inundation of the Nile would start at around this time, making the soil fertile enough for the growing of all the food that kept Egyptians alive. Spells were cast and prayers said to encourage an abundance of water. The festival involved sacrifices of sheep, goats and cattle as well as human effigies.

The Beautiful Feast of the Valley was a commemoration of the dead and had a personal aspect, with individuals and families offering tributes to and visiting the tombs of their ancestors (especially in the Valley of the Kings) where feasts would also be held. This event was crucial to maintaining continuity between the world of the living and that of the departed.

The Opet Festival of Thebes was perhaps the largest and most vibrant of all. Its purpose was to celebrate the sacred marriage between the god Amun and his consort Mut. Statues of these two and their son Khonsu

would be carried in a procession from the grand temple in Karnak to the one in Luxor, representing the rejuvenation of supernatural authority. Massive crowds would attend this festival, eating, drinking and enjoying the dancing and music-making. Incense and essential oils would be burned en masse, which must have been somewhat intoxicating for the revellers.

ANY EXCUSE FOR A PARTY

We can get a sense of the hedonism of Egyptian festival-goers from a ritual at Opet in which the pharaoh would quaff beer to denote his symbolic marriage to Hathor. Though it sounds like an unconvincing excuse to us nowadays, the rationale then was that the beer stimulated certain holy forces inside the pharaoh, boosting his capacity to govern and defend the kingdom.

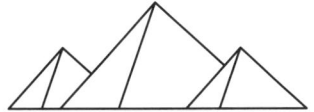

THE OLDEST EGYPTIAN
HISTORICAL RECORD

One surviving artefact that has much to tell us about the early artistic flourishing of Ancient Egypt is the Narmer Palette, now housed in the Egyptian Museum in Cairo. Made from siltstone and standing at 64 cm (2 feet) tall, it was made in the First Dynasty in the Early Dynastic Period. Its bas-relief carvings show the unification of Upper and Lower Egypt under King Narmer.

There is an intriguing symmetry to the illustrations. On one side of the palette, Narmer is depicted donning the White Crown of Upper Egypt as he strikes an adversary (possibly a Libyan) with his mace, a symbol of royal authority, in the process of annexing Lower Egypt. On the other side, Narmer can be seen wearing the Red Crown of Lower Egypt, signifying his supremacy over both regions.

On the palette are also references to the Nile and the papyrus plant – two essential facets of early Ancient Egyptian culture. Stranger still is an image of two men gripping ropes attached to the interlocking necks of two serpopards facing one another. The serpopard was a mythical beast, a fearsome hybrid of a snake and a leopard.

RAISING THE GLASS

During the same epoch that saw the construction of the Narmer Palette, Ancient Egyptian craftspeople developed a distinctive glass-like material called faience. Faience is made from silica (oxide of silicon), small quantities of soda and lime, and a colourant, often copper. The material was used to produce lustrous tiles, beads, figurines and other wares.

A brightly coloured amulet depicting a fish and covered with faience came to be a sought-after possession, affording spiritual protection to the living when worn round the neck and to the dead when placed inside their tombs.

The Egyptians were famed for their technical prowess not only in making glassware but for adding trace elements to influence its hue. A variation on the faience recipe yielded blue frit, perhaps the world's first synthetic pigment. It gave a gentle and alluring blue tone to faience as well as to pottery, plaster, wood, stone and papyri. In addition, Egyptians could produce a spectrum of other pigments including red, yellow, purple and white.

STRENGTH IN NUMBERS

Many Ancient Egyptian cultural achievements were underpinned by the civilization's discoveries in mathematics. Their system, developed in around 3000 BCE, was rooted in fractions that were expressed as sums of fractions with a numerator of 1 (e.g. 1/2, 1/3, 1/4). Their decimal system was based on 10, with hieroglyphs denoting powers of 10 (1, 10, 100, 1,000 and so forth). There was no symbol for zero. In addition, the Egyptians devised new techniques for addition, subtraction, division and multiplication.

The pyramids stand as the greatest tribute to, among other things, Egyptian numeracy. Engineers and architects had figured out and applied the principles of Pythagoras' theorem long before the Greek polymath was born. Ratios and right angles were essential to getting the proportions of other monuments right, as was the invention of the Egyptian cubit, a unit of measurement.

The precision and symmetry of smaller-scale artistic compositions such as tomb friezes are thought to have been influenced by Egyptian leaps forward. These also made the business of landscaping gardens and establishing land boundaries that much easier.

GRAND DESIGNS

Aside from the genius evident in the creation of pyramids, Egyptian architecture was extraordinarily advanced and varied. At 247 acres the temple complex of Karnak is arguably the biggest edifice of its kind on Earth, striking for its Hypostyle Hall at the heart of its Great Temple of Amun. The hall's columns are colossal and notable for their fluted surfaces and capitals (tops). The Luxor Temple is best known architecturally for its enormous pylons (gateways) around the grand entrance. Luxor's inner sanctum and open-air square were designed to allow sunlight to flood in during the time of the Opet Festival.

The rock-cut tombs in the Valley of the Kings are remarkable feats given the rudimentary tools available to the builders. Copper chisels and stone hammers would be used to carve an entrance shaft and connecting chambers out of the rock. Understandably, the process could take decades.

Obelisks were unique tower-like structures with four sides and a tapered top. They symbolized the sun god Ra and were most commonly built near temple entrances.

ALTERNATIVE WORSHIP

While the main temples of Ancient Egypt were blessed and controlled by the state, there was at the same time a multiplicity of obscure and unofficial cults. These often involved esoteric initiation rituals, sacrifices and eccentric ceremonies.

For those who wanted to risk it, the Crocodile Cult of Fayum required members to tame and feed crocodiles, and sometimes to adorn them with jewellery. The Bastet cult in Bubastis took the same approach to cats.

SEX CULTS

Zealous followers of Hathor, the goddess of love and fertility, were required to dance erotically, paint pictures of deities in sexual poses and even participate in ritual orgies. Although there is no consensus, some scholars hold that religious prostitution took place at certain Hathor temples, with priestesses having sex with male cultists to summon the goddess's goodwill. Devotees of Min, another fertility deity, ate lettuce as an aphrodisiac. It was believed that the way its stalks emerged from the soil brought to mind a particular part of a man's anatomy...

PICTURE THIS

As with so much else in Ancient Egyptian culture, portraiture in the civilization was focused on honouring and preserving the identities of individuals so that they would have the best chances of reaching the afterlife.

Only pharaohs and VIPs tended to be painted and, in the Old and Middle Kingdom periods, were normally depicted in a formal, stylized pose, expressing the personage's sacred character rather than their actual appearance. Ramses II, for example, was still being portrayed as young, fit and muscular even when he was well into his 60-year reign. However, realism started to influence Egyptian portrait art in the New Kingdom and Ptolemaic epochs, epitomized by funerary illustrations.

Pharaohs had a vested interest in being rendered as regal and authoritative, their beards, crowns, maces and luxury clothing prominent in their pictures. Noblemen and women were often depicted in similar grand terms, their stations in life and the afterlife alluded to through costumes and objects relating to their expertise and status.

MIXING IT ALL UP

Given that Ancient Egyptian civilization lasted for so long, it was inevitable that religious beliefs and artistic practices would increasingly be influenced by other cultures. The process was often a compromise between the imperative to uphold local customs and the pressure to adapt and embrace the new and foreign.

Egypt's encounters with the Nubians, Greeks and Romans produced hybrid deities. After the Kushite invasion, which heralded the start of the Twenty-fifth Dynasty, the Kushite kings adopted the Egyptian god Amun. This was probably for political reasons but they gave him a distinctly Nubian identity, portraying him with African features such as curly hair and darker skin.

During and after the Ptolemaic dynasty, the Egyptian goddess Hathor was merged with the Greek goddess Aphrodite, later known as Venus by the Romans. Horus, originally a Greek deity, rose to prominence in the Egyptian pantheon at this time.

Cultural influence was a two-way street, however, with the realist turn in Egyptian painting likely influenced by Greek culture, while in turn later influencing Roman cultural achievements such as the Fayum mummy portraits.

BATTLE OF THE STICKS

Likely first played in the Old Kingdom, Ancient Egyptian stick fighting was unique to that civilization and is known today as *tahtib*. It was not a sport as we would understand the term today but rather a mish-mash of martial art, ritual dance and military training method.

Players duelled with one another using four-foot-long wooden sticks. Like sword fighting and fencing practised in later civilizations, the aim was to land blows on your opponent using agility and footwork. These contests were accompanied by flutes and drums, suggesting a dimension of choreography to the proceedings.

Stick fighting later evolved into a more stylized and performative discipline and was particularly popular in Upper Egypt. In tomb paintings of the New Kingdom era, performers are seen striking flamboyant poses in the middle of a fight, implying that these events were not especially competitive or adversarial.

Contemporary *tahtib* has been categorized by UNESCO as an Intangible Cultural Heritage and continues to be performed in present-day Egypt but more as a ceremonial dance, with participants twirling their sticks in elaborate moves.

A WORLD OF WIGS

It's doubtful that wigs would have taken off elsewhere in the world had the Egyptians not pioneered their production and use. Men and women alike wore them, though upper-class and priestly types were more likely to don hairpieces than poorer Egyptians.

Wigs had several uses. They denoted high status, blocked the harsh North African sun from vulnerable scalps and helped Egyptians to look elegant and attractive. Wigs were mostly made from human hair or plant fibres and were interwoven with jewels and beads.

If you thought hairstyles were a more recent invention, Egyptian wigs were available in all shapes, sizes and lengths. Flat-tops, braids, curls and partings were all popular. Wigs were also believed to bring the wearer closer to the gods and were placed on the heads of mummies to ensure they looked good upon arrival to the afterlife and would be judged favourably.

Rather than wear wigs, it seems that Ancient Egyptian children shaved their heads, noble ones leaving just a long lock of hair on the left side of their head. This was called "a sidelock of youth" and denoted an intimate connection with the god Osiris.

THE HEALING POWER OF NATURE

Ancient Egyptians were keen gardeners and loved to spend time in green spaces, which were thought to convey a sense of the bucolic atmosphere of the afterlife. Lower-class Egyptians had access to communal areas of land on the banks of the Nile and elsewhere, where they could relax. Temple gardens were open to all and tended by priests who grew plants in honour of the gods. The lotus, a cipher for fertility and rebirth, was associated with the genesis of Egyptian civilization, as a myth describes Ra being born from this flower.

The most pleasant gardens were privately owned and reflected the prosperity and privilege of upper-class Egyptians. In addition to the plants mentioned above, these spaces had fig trees, date palms and doum palms (linked to the god Thoth) often irrigated by channels or pools fed by the Nile. Elite Egyptians would meditate in or stroll around their gardens.

A poem from the Twentieth Dynasty describes the garden as a place where young people could consume alcohol and enjoy themselves: "Her companion is on her right, While she is making him drunk..."

A LASTING LEGACY

We've seen how Ancient Egypt achieved its greatness and what day-to-day life was like there. But what does all this add up to for those of us, all over the world, who have come after that extraordinary civilization? For one thing, pharaohs, tombs and pyramids maintain a firm grip over our imaginations, and have inspired countless novels, movies, TV series and computer games. But did you know that Egypt has also influenced modern languages, music, architecture, furniture design, cosmetics, postal services and thinking about political liberation – as well as, more troublingly, some of our most eccentric conspiracy theories? Curious? Then read on.

THE LEGACY OF TUTANKHAMUN

Few aspects of Ancient Egypt have cast such a long
shadow over modern popular culture as Tutankhamun,
a pharaoh who ruled in the Eighteenth Dynasty in
the New Kingdom period. His golden funerary mask
is one of the most famous images of Ancient Egypt,
often serving as a symbol of the entire civilization. Like
many icons, Tutankhamun has become better known
in death than for his achievements while alive (see page
32). Adding to the mystique is his premature death,
aged just 18, possibly from a combination of a fractured
leg and malaria.

He was mummified and entombed, along with many
valuable artefacts, in the eastern branch of the Valley of
the Kings. His tomb was robbed twice in the first few
years after his death, and Egyptian officials repaired
some of the damage. It is likely that his resting place
was protected from further infiltration by a build-up of
alluvium resulting from flooding during Pharaoh Ay's
reign (*c.* 1323–1319 BCE).

In 1907–1909 CE, Western Egyptologists unearthed
objects related to Tutankhamun in the valley. In 1922
CE, archaeologist Howard Carter, backed financially by
Lord Carnarvon, located and entered the tomb proper.

Carter and his colleagues found a trove of artefacts, including Tutankhamun's stone-carved sarcophagus, lavish shrines, a meteorite dagger, ivory board games, over thirty walking sticks and the late pharaoh's embalmed organs in jars.

The finds triggered a global media frenzy and "King Tut", as he was christened by the press, was invoked in film, literature, advertising, fashion, art and architecture.

THE CURSE OF KING TUT

As recounted in Hollywood movies like *The Mummy* (1932) and TV series such as *Tutankhamun* (2016), those involved in uncovering the tomb supposedly fell under a curse. Reportedly, a cobra – an emblem of Egyptian royalty – stole into Carter's house and savaged his pet canary. When Lord Carnarvon died from an infected mosquito bite in 1923, newspapers claimed this was Tutankhamun's revenge. It was probably just bad luck: of the 58 people who were at the first sighting of the tomb, only eight perished within a dozen years.

MEDICAL DEBTS

Long before us, the Ancient Egyptians understood how infection worked, applying honey as an antiseptic to wounds and wrapping them in sterilized bandages. They also knew the health benefits of garlic, aloe vera, acacia and willow bark (a precursor to the aspirin we use today). The *Ebers Papyrus* (see page 44) details more than 800 pharmacological treatments, many of which have been proven by modern science to work.

Modern surgery owes a good deal to Egyptian techniques for amputation and draining abscesses. Egyptian physicians set broken bones with splints, allowing them to heal properly, and crafted prosthetic limbs – a wooden toe discovered on a mummy confirms this.

The Egyptian flair for writing and record-keeping meant that illnesses and treatments were methodically documented, allowing physicians to share best practice and ensuring a legacy to help future doctors and dentists.

Although Egypt was a deeply religious society, care was taken to analyze cause and effect in a rigorous way that prefigured the scientific method.

The *Edwin Smith Papyrus* from the Second Intermediate Period avoids talk of the supernatural

and instead demonstrates precocious knowledge of the workings of the brain and nervous system. It documents 48 real-life cases of injuries to the spine, head, limbs and other parts of the body and proposes treatments that would appear sensible to us today, such as suturing and bandaging.

The Egyptians knew how to extract teeth and reinforce wobbly teeth with gold wire, methods that will be familiar to present-day dentists. Way before us, they were rinsing their mouths with natural antiseptics like salt and applying clove oil to combat gum pain.

While the Egyptian recipe for toothpaste – including pepper, rock salt and irises – might not be something we would want to put in our mouths, the Egyptians pioneered the use of mint in these concoctions, and that custom, at least, remains with us. They also invented breath fresheners consisting of boiled honey and cinnamon, frankincense and myrrh.

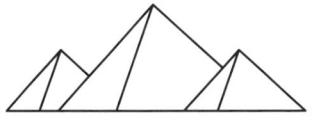

THE MOTHER OF ALL LANGUAGES

The 24 uniliteral signs of Egyptian hieroglyphics formed the basis of all future alphabets across the globe. They emerged in the Early Dynastic time and begat the Proto-Sinaitic script, written and spoken by Semitic-speaking populations in the Sinai Peninsula. This evolved into the Phoenician alphabet, the direct precursor of Greek, Latin and our contemporary alphabets.

Our modern word for "paper" is derived from "papyrus", with the Egyptians being the first to make such a material and commit text to it. The production process – strips of the papyrus stalk stuck together using the plant's sap – was shared with other cultures through travel and trade, eventually influencing the Chinese, who made the first paper in 100 BCE.

INK, INC.

Ancient Egyptians were the first to produce ink on a large scale, concocting it from carbon black, the result of burning oil or wood and gathering the soot generated. Water was added to the soot to produce a black paste-like substance that was used for writing.

POST-HASTE

Ancient Egypt may not have developed the first mail delivery system, but it did make breakthroughs in the field. A network of couriers – a sub-profession of the scribe class – conveyed messages all over the kingdom on foot, by donkey or by skiff along the Nile to the major cities.

The Egyptians probably did invent the official letter, however, using wax or clay to seal documents written on papyri. Wooden tablets or *ostraca* (shards of pottery) were also sent out to relate political decrees, taxation demands and religious diktats. Temples served as de facto post offices, with priests and administrators sorting, sending and receiving correspondence.

The Egyptian military had its own communication set-up, and orders and requests between senior officers were relayed by runners and horsemen.

BEFORE SOCIAL MEDIA RAGE THERE WAS...

In 2020, Egyptologist Deborah Sweeney discovered letters that exhibited anger and hurt felt between Ancient Egyptians. In one, a scribe asked a friend, "What offence have I done against you?" and accused him of what we would call ghosting today.

LOANWORDS

A few dozen Ancient Egyptian words have entered the English language in the millennia since that great civilization fell. Others have come to us via Greek and Latin mutations.

As you would expect, the English word "pharaoh" is closely based on the Egyptian "per-aa", meaning "palace" or "great house". It later came to mean the ruler of Egypt. *Hbny* was adapted to "ebony" in reference to the tree. The name Susan or Susana derives from the word *sšn* meaning "lotus flower".

While Ancient Egyptians used *kŏtŏn* to signify the plant rather than the textile fibre, which is what the English "cotton" normally means, clearly the latter word was informed by the former.

Curiously, the word "pyramid", which refers to that quintessentially Ancient Egyptian structure, comes to us second-hand via the Greek *pyramis*, itself rooted in the Egyptian *per-em-us*. "Alcohol" relates to the Arabic word *al-kuḥl* but ultimately reaches back to the Egyptian *kohl* (also meaning a powdered substance applied as eye make-up).

ANCIENT EGYPT AND BLACK LIBERATION

Beginning in the nineteenth century CE, African American writers, artists and activists drew on Ancient Egypt as a cultural resource for their own struggles for civil rights and political emancipation.

In opposition to the white supremacism of their time, community leaders such as Marcus Garvey and, later, Malcolm X regarded Ancient Egypt as proof that Black people had founded a powerful and sophisticated civilization. After the discovery of Tutankhamun's tomb, Garvey's wife, Amy Jacques Garvey, wrote: "The exponents of white superiority cannot claim him as their own, [so] they make no comment as to his racial stock."

In 1921, Langston Hughes, leading light of the Harlem Renaissance in literature, wrote his classic poem "The Negro Speaks of Rivers", which makes an explicit connection between the African American experience and the Nile River of antiquity.

Visual artists including Jean-Michel Basquiat, Kara Walker and the Afrofuturists incorporated hieroglyphics and pharaonic symbols into their works, while the academic Scott Trafton has chronicled the influence of Ancient Egypt on African American thought and culture in his book *Egypt Land* (2004).

SHAPING OUR FAITHS

Egypt's religious revolution under Pharaoh Akhenaten (see pages 27–28) made it the first civilization to be monotheistic. The notion of a single, omnipotent, omnipresent deity influenced the major religions of our own day, primarily Christianity, Judaism and Islam.

Ancient Egypt's polytheistic era and certain of its numerous deities have also left a strong legacy. Scholars claim that the god Osiris, who was re-born after being slain by his brother Set, must have influenced early Christian theologians, especially in the narrative of Jesus Christ's life, death and resurrection. Jesus' virgin birth was nothing new either: Horus' mother, Isis, was a virgin, supposedly.

Egyptian ideas of alternative afterlives, depending on how well one had behaved in life, fed into Jewish, Islamic and Christian beliefs about heaven, hell and final judgement.

THE COMEBACK?

Not without controversy, Tamara Siuda created the Kemetic movement to try to revive Egyptian religion. In 1996, she spent time in the temples at Karnak and Luxor and had herself "crowned" as a latter-day pharaoh.

CULTS AND THE OCCULT

Over the last couple of centuries, fringe beliefs in black magic, curses and the supernatural have borrowed liberally from Ancient Egyptian religion, although not always faithfully. Founded in 1717 CE, the secret society of Freemasonry draws on pyramid imagery in its all-seeing eye motif, which represents knowledge, holy providence and moral uprightness. The Masons also invoked the mysterious Sphinx.

The Russian mystic Helena Blavatsky (1831–1891 CE) founded theosophy, a spiritual discipline that referenced Egyptian gods in its explication of an esoteric system of knowledge that underpinned the material world.

First published in 1908 CE, *The Kybalion* proposed that consciousness constructed the world in a tribute to Ancient Egyptian Hermetic philosophy. Occultist showman Aleister Crowley's (1875–1947 CE) libertarian "do what thou wilt" creed was, he claimed, derived from the *Book of the Law* that he said was given to him by a mystical being called Aiwass in Cairo in 1904. Crowley's self-made religion incorporated Nuit, goddess of the sky, along with other Ancient Egyptian deities.

COGNIZANT OF THE COSMOS

The Egyptians knew a lot about celestial bodies, tracking time by observing the movements of the stars and the sun. This led them to the conclusion that there should be a 24-hour day, with 12 hours of daylight and 12 hours of night. The Ancient Greeks and Romans adopted this structure and it is still with us today.

Without Ancient Egyptian breakthroughs in timekeeping, our modern calendars might never have been invented. The Egyptians were among the first to devise a solar calendar that had years of 365 days, divided into 12 months of 30 days apiece, with five extra days added to align the year with the sun's cycle. The calendar was based on the annual ascent of the star Sirius, which was linked to the goddess Isis, when the flooding of the Nile River would begin.

Our contemporary clocks and watches were heavily influenced by Egyptian sundials and *clepsydrae* (water clocks), stone pots with a hole in the bottom into which liquid would be poured.

WHAT DID THE EGYPTIANS EVER BUILD FOR US?

Successive civilizations have learned a substantial amount about architecture and engineering from the Ancient Egyptians. Their management and execution of the building of large-scale monuments remains impressive. Their application of load-bearing walls in pyramids and temples has been imitated ever since, and our contemporary cranes used for carrying large materials have their origins in Ancient Egyptian levers and ramps.

Today, when a building is erected on unstable ground, foundation engineering methods must be used. Many of them were pioneered by the Egyptians. Many grand buildings of today, from city halls to parliament buildings and from universities to libraries, feature columns and obelisks that look and feel much like their Egyptian counterparts.

The phases of Western neoclassical (late eighteenth/ early nineteenth centuries CE) and modernist architecture (early to mid-twentieth century CE) deployed the same kinds of intricate decorations and symmetries.

A more recent invention of ours, the eco-home, has, nonetheless, been shaped by the Egyptian use of mud-brick walls to ensure natural insulation.

THEY HAD THE PYRAMIDS, WE HAVE...

The ambition and style of Egyptian pyramid- and temple-building has inspired several iconic structures around the contemporary world.

The Capitol Building in Washington, DC, is something of a homage to the pyramids with its grandiose domes and columns. Nearby, the 152 m (500 feet) tall Washington Monument could be mistaken for an Egyptian obelisk and commemorates a figure equivalent in status to any pharaoh: the first president of the republic, George Washington.

New York's Chrysler Building makes wonderful use of sunburst patterns and fluted columns, architectural techniques the Egyptians perfected millennia before its construction in 1929–1931. More faithful to pyramid design are Albania's Pyramid of Tirana, a stepped concrete affair erected in 1988, and Paris's glass pyramid in the Louvre Museum.

EGYPTIAN PARODY

The ostentatious Luxor Hotel & Casino in Las Vegas, USA, comprises a dark glass pyramid, a model sphinx and a "Sky Beam" that projects the brightest light in the world.

STATE OF THE ART

Ancient Egyptian art started to cast its shadow over its Western counterpart in the nineteenth century, following Napoleon's Egyptian campaign and the unearthing of the Rosetta Stone.

After the discovery of Tutankhamun's tomb in 1922, the then-current Art Deco movement began to incorporate geometric shapes, sharp lines and stylized depictions of humans and animals into its works. Cubism and surrealism borrowed Egyptian motifs and techniques, with artists like Pablo Picasso imitating the minimalism and boldness of antiquity.

Today, no realm of visual culture has been left untouched by Egyptian art – from graphic design to tattoos, fashion and advertising.

EVERYDAY VESSELS

In our modern world vases are found in almost every home. Their manufacture has its origins in the Ancient Egyptian method of immersing sand moulds into molten glass and pressing the result onto a chilled slab. The earliest Egyptian vases date to the time of Pharaoh Thutmose III (reign: 1492–1479 BCE).

EGYPT BETWEEN THE PAGES

Novelists have long been setting their stories in the dramatic and mysterious world of Ancient Egypt. Here are some of the best.

H. RIDER HAGGARD, *CLEOPATRA: BEING AN ACCOUNT OF THE FALL AND VENGEANCE OF HARMACHIS* (1889)

From the pioneering adventure novelist who wrote *King Solomon's Mines*, this early fictional account of "The Queen of Kings" blends historical detail with fantastical events.

NAGUIB MAHFOUZ, *KHUFU'S WISDOM* (1939)

This gripping yarn by modern Egypt's finest writer concerns the turmoil created by the emergence of a prophecy about the fall of the Khufu dynasty.

MIKA WALTARI, *THE EGYPTIAN* (1945)

The hero of this story is a physician named Sinuhe, and through him the reader learns about Egyptian intrigue, religion and daily life.

ANNE RICE, *THE MUMMY, OR RAMSES THE DAMNED* (1989)

Best known for her chilling, Southern Gothic work *Interview with the Vampire*, Rice delivers an imaginative and provocative tale about an Ancient Egyptian cleric who is resurrected in the present day.

PAULINE GEDGE, *HOUSE OF DREAMS* (1994)

A young girl flees from her poverty-stricken village in the Nile Delta to become a healer and royal concubine. A tale of passion, envy and manipulation, *House of Dreams* also conveys a vivid impression of the rigid Ancient Egyptian class system.

WILBUR SMITH, *WARLOCK* (2001)

One of the biggest-selling authors in history, the British South African Smith has penned a series of engrossing novels set in Ancient Egypt. This one centres on Taita, an intelligent and wily former slave.

MICHELLE MORAN, *NEFERTITI* (2007)

This dramatic reconstruction of one of the great female pharaohs has drawn plaudits for its historical accuracy.

EGYPT ON THE BIG SCREEN

Egypt's majesty, scale and mystery have long been well-suited to Hollywood's tastes. These are some of the standout films.

THE TEN COMMANDMENTS (1956)
DIRECTED BY CECIL B. DEMILLE

The most famous film to have been set in Ancient Egypt, this special-effects-driven epic concerns the protagonist Moses (played by Charlton Heston) who starts out as a courtier of the pharaoh before leading the Israelites to the promised land.

CLEOPATRA (1963) DIRECTED BY JOSEPH L. MANKIEWICZ

More concerned with human relationships than other "swords and sandals" productions, *Cleopatra* stars Elizabeth Taylor as the titular queen and Richard Burton as her lover Mark Antony. The film performed badly at the box office but impressed critics with its sumptuous sets and costumes.

THE PRINCE OF EGYPT (1998) DIRECTED BY BRENDA CHAPMAN, SIMON WELLS AND STEVE HICKNER

This DreamWorks animation focuses on the relationship between Moses and Pharaoh Ramses. It was lauded for its emotional depth, making it appealing to all ages.

THE MUMMY (1999) DIRECTED BY STEPHEN SOMMERS

A fast-paced adventure, *The Mummy* eschews authenticity for sometimes very silly action and horror scenes. In the 1920s, a party of Western Egyptologists, led by a breathless Brendan Fraser, accidentally stirs a mummified cleric and all hell breaks loose.

THE SCORPION KING (2002) DIRECTED BY CHUCK RUSSELL

Helping cement the fame of the actor Dwayne "The Rock" Johnson, this sort-of-sequel to *The Mummy* is similarly fantastical and thrill-packed and charts the ascent of a fearsome warrior in Ancient Egypt.

EXODUS: GODS AND KINGS (2014) DIRECTED BY RIDLEY SCOTT

This latest iteration of the Moses–Ramses duel mobilized CGI to bring the majesty and mysticism of the time and place alive. The performances of Christian Bale and Joel Edgerton received particular praise from critics.

EGYPT ON THE SMALL SCREEN

The longevity of its dynasties and the intricacies of its politics have made Ancient Egypt an apt subject of longer-form TV series since the 1960s.

HORUS: PRINCE OF THE SUN (1968)

Featuring the skills of Hayao Miyazaki, who would later find superstardom with his Studio Ghibli, *Horus* is a Japanese anime that dramatizes the eponymous deity's quest to destroy the forces of evil.

THE CLEOPATRAS (1983)

This classy BBC series related the stories of each of the seven Cleopatras who reigned in Egypt and was more historically accurate than other TV treatments. It starred the Shakespearean actor Robert Hardy as Mark Antony.

ANCIENT EGYPTIANS (2003–4)

A painstakingly researched and highly informative docudrama that included dramatic reconstructions of key persons and events in Egypt's history.

MELODIES FROM THE NILE

As we have seen, music was as central to Ancient Egyptian life as it is to our own. The tunes of ancient times have helped shape the tunes of more recent times.

As part of the Egyptomania of the nineteenth century CE, acclaimed European composers such as Camille Saint-Saëns and Verdi incorporated Egyptian-inflected harmonies into their operas. The antique civilization's Phrygian and harmonic minor scales can be heard in the tonalities of our rock, metal and electronica genres, while the intricate polyrhythms of Egyptian drumming inspired jazz and funk musicians from Sun Ra to George Clinton. Some of the most iconic album covers of the 1970s and 80s, such as Pink Floyd's *Dark Side of the Moon* (1973) and Iron Maiden's *Powerslave* (1984), feature hieroglyphics, temples, pyramids and pharaohs. Artists in the electronic realm, from Vangelis to Jean-Michel Jarre, have tried to emulate the atmospherics of Ancient Egyptian music, while hip-hop and R&B tracks including Beyoncé's "Formation" and Mos Def's "Mathematics" have made explicit reference to Egyptian themes and images.

DIGITAL EGYPT

Ancient Egypt has enthralled computer game programmers since the earliest days of the form.

In *Tomb Raider: The Last Revelation* (1999), the player controls daring archaeologist Lara Croft in an exploration of Egyptian tombs and ruins. The same year saw the release of *Pharaoh*, in which the aim is to macro-manage Egyptian civilization, erecting monuments and fighting neighbouring empires.

Somewhat zanier is *Immortal Redneck* (2017), which eschews historical realism for a surreal shoot-'em-up experience inside something resembling the Pyramid of Giza. 2023's *Sphinx and the Cursed Mummy* is a role-playing game romp around mythical creatures and magical portals.

AN EARLY GEM

Regarded as one of the first titles in the shooter genre, *Total Eclipse* (1988) has an intriguing premise: an archaeologist in 1930 discovers that a curse will cause a total eclipse to obstruct the sun above Cairo and destroy the world. You must sneak into a pyramid and avert the curse by destroying a shrine to Ra.

BOWLING FOR CONCUBINES

Over 45 million people a year go bowling in the USA, but the sport's origins could be from the east. In Naqada, Egypt, in 1899 CE, British Egyptologist Sir William Matthew Flinders Petrie located an Ancient Egyptian infant's grave from the Predynastic Period containing pins and marbles. His theory? This was a primitive bowling set.

Elsewhere, archaeologists found different-sized balls and a lane with a hole in the middle, which some balls were small enough to fall through while others were not. That the Roman Egyptians played a similar game, as indicated by balls and a 4 m (13 feet) long lane excavated in Cairo, suggests that the rules of bowling in times of antiquity were quite different to our modern regulations, even if the former probably evolved into the latter.

Egyptian balls were often made of husks of corn, coated with leather and held together with string, but could also be constructed from porcelain or stone.

MADE UP FOR US

Skincare regimes and beauty trends might seem the essence of advanced modern society. However, as with so many other things, the Egyptians got there first.

Ancient Egyptians cleaned and moisturized their skin with milk, honey and aloe vera – ingredients still found in today's products. Then, as now, clay masks and salt scrubs were used to head off the effects of ageing and generally keep people looking beautiful. In addition, Cleopatra was known to bathe in goat's milk, while others preferred sugar scrubs – the precursor to modern-day spa treatments.

Egyptians loved their bold dark eyeliner, making it from charcoal, soot, galena (lead sulphide) or malachite (green copper carbonate). They pioneered the smoky cat's eye and winged eyeliner styles that are still popular today.

Our fondness for lipstick and blush can be traced back to the Egyptian custom of applying scarlet ochre, beetroot and carmine (crushed beetles) to their mouths and cheeks. If you thought aromatherapy and essential oils were a New Age innovation, the Egyptians were making natural perfumes from myrrh, jasmine and frankincense way before we were all born.

THE BODY AS A TEMPLE

In the late twentieth and early twenty-first centuries CE, tattoos grew in popularity in the Western world. Painting one's nails has been popular for some time. But the Egyptians were into all this thousands of years ago – and we are still using their methods.

A means of spiritual protection, tattoos were more common on Ancient Egyptian women than on men. Priestesses had images of deities like Isis, while dancers went for motifs related to fertility, purity and healing. Mummies have been found with tattoos of dots, discs and lotus flowers. All these symbols have remained popular in body art all over the world.

We use henna (a natural dye made from the *Lawsonia inermis* plant) today largely because the Egyptians blazed the trail by applying it to their nails. The darker the shade, the higher your status, generally speaking.

HEAD AND SHOULDERS ABOVE

Barbers and hairdressers are ubiquitous on our high streets today and guess who we have to thank for them? The world's first tonsorial stylists were operating in the Predynastic Period. Men were employed to trim and groom the hair and beard using shells and sharpened flints. Fashions changed, just like they do nowadays, and clean-shaven might be trendy one year, hirsuteness the next.

Since early barbering was seen to have a spiritual and medical benefit, clergymen and physicians doubled as hairdressers. Later in the development of Egypt such work became specialized and professionalized, with barbers highly trained and as well-regarded as craftspeople.

If you were rich you'd likely have your own live-in hairdresser or a regular one who called at your home. However, ordinary Egyptians would have to visit one of the city's street-level barbers – a tradition that persists today.

SITTING COMFORTABLY?

Of all modern-day items that we might take for granted, the humble table and chair might be two of them. That said, there is evidence implying that, before the Egyptians, humans tended to sit on the floor, on stools or on simple benches. But in the Early Dynastic era artisans began building more and more furniture out of wood and alabaster. These items included certain smooth platforms held up by legs or a pedestal, and similar constructions with soft seats, armrests and high backs. Sound familiar?

Early tables performed the same sorts of functions as our modern tables do. People ate off them, wrote on them and played board games at them.

Chairs were enjoyed as a status symbol by the elite, who had them made from sumptuous materials like ivory and ebony and decorated them with gold and silver. Carvings of gods and animals were also popular. The middle classes made do with simpler affairs, while farm workers and slaves sat on stools.

NAPOLEON IN EGYPT

As part of his imperial expansion of France, Napoleon Bonaparte (1769–1824 CE) occupied Egypt between 1798 and 1801 CE. His formidable army brought with it 167 botanists, historians, lexicographers, engineers and other learned men to study Ancient Egypt with unprecedented rigour. Europeans were able to learn about Egypt's ancient monuments, culture and geography for the first time. The great Palestinian philosopher Edward Said (1935–2003 CE) claimed that the project's real aim was to use Western knowledge as a form of colonial control over the Orient.

Napoleon's scholars and scientists recorded their findings in the 23-volume *Description de l'Égypte*, which took 20 years to compile. Napoleon's campaign caused an upsurge in European public interest in the civilization and laid the groundwork for the discipline of Egyptology.

A LIE REPEATED

Contrary to a popular myth, a French cannon did not shoot the Sphinx's nose off in 1798. Its absence predated Napoleon by perhaps 300 years.

THE THIN BLUE NILE

One of the lesser-known legacies of Ancient Egypt is organized policing. As its metropolises developed into places of intense commerce and competition, so crime burgeoned and, by the time of the Fourth Dynasty of the Old Kingdom, the state decided something had to be done about it.

A basic police force was established to patrol vessels on the River Nile, defending them from pirates and thieves. By the Eighteenth Dynasty of the New Kingdom, an elite gendarmerie called the Medjay was in operation, tasked with protecting the pharaoh's possessions and providing security in his palace, capital city and along Egypt's borders.

Egyptian law enforcement carried out duties more akin to our present-day uniformed police, apprehending felons using dogs and even baboons (see page 71). Unlike our cops today, they could summarily punish offenders – and often brutally. They did not conduct any detective work, not least because victims or prosecutors in criminal cases had to gather all their own evidence, according to the kingdom's laws.

UNDER LOCK AND KEY

Anyone who wasn't a pharaoh, and thus couldn't depend on direct police protection, had a plan B: securing their property with the Egyptian tumbler lock, a device that is very familiar to us today. It consisted of a lock containing several pins that were lifted by prongs when a matching key was inserted and turned. This allowed a central bolt to be pulled back and the door opened. For its time, this was a huge step forward in the field of engineering and prefigured our more complicated key-and-lock mechanisms of today.

Early tumbler locks could be 60 cm (2 feet) long, suggesting that Egyptians took guarding their possessions rather seriously. This is also evidenced by the severe punishments that tomb robbers were subject to (see page 58). As with the furniture and best cosmetics developed in Ancient Egyptian times, however, locks were only for the better-off and have even been found inside the great pyramids.

"PYRAMIDOLOGY"

The abiding centrality of Ancient Egypt in our popular imagination has resulted in some peculiar pseudoscientific theories about the "true" purposes of the pyramids. With the evidence not on their side, Graham Hancock and others have posited the use of sonic technology, levitation, psychokinesis or the summoning of gods to help with the lifting of mammoth stone blocks when building the pyramids. Another unlikely speculation is that the Egyptians were the direct descendants of the lost civilization of Atlantis.

Others have claimed that if we could "properly" understand the wall paintings and architectural features of the Great Pyramid of Giza, we would unlock all the secrets of religions that were to develop afterwards, including Judaism and Christianity.

SPREADING YOUR BETS

Some pyramidologists have argued that Giza is encoded with predictions for the start of World War One in 1914 CE, the foundation of the modern state of Israel in 1948 CE, global warming and climate change, and the end of the world in 2012 CE.

ALIENS AND ELECTRICITY

Another unorthodox theory, advanced in Christopher Dunn's book *The Giza Power Plant* (1998), holds that the Giza pyramid could attract and transmit electrical energy. This, Dunn asserted, was why Giza's design was aligned with the stars and the sun and was constructed user super-tough materials like granite. The pyramid was thus a colossal machine that generated and amplified energy via the piezoelectric qualities of its materials.

Other "scholars" have suggested that extraterrestrial visitors may have given the Egyptians the know-how they needed to establish such a power source. Erich von Däniken's 1968 book *Chariots of the Gods?* alleged that the pyramids were, in fact, landing sites for spaceships that transported aliens to Earth.

To be sure, orthodox Egyptologists and historians reject these pseudohistorical ideas, since no hard evidence has ever been provided to back them up. In some ways, such conspiracy theories are insulting to the Egyptians, implying that they couldn't have possibly built their great monuments by themselves. But the fact that these dubious ideas endure is a testament to the romantic appeal Ancient Egypt continues to have in the minds of many.

ONGOING DISCOVERIES

The thrill of Egyptology is that we are learning more and more about its subject matter as time goes on, solving mysteries that have baffled researchers for millennia.

For years archaeologists were searching for the tombs of the early Eighteenth Dynasty pharaohs. Thutmose II's mummy had been excavated in 1881 CE but its original burial place had eluded the best minds in the business. They speculated that the site was near the Valley of the Kings.

Then, in early 2025, a British–Egyptian team found it more than 2 km (1.2 miles) away, near the city of Luxor in the Western Valleys of the Theban Necropolis. After crawling through a narrow passage, they entered a subterranean chamber with a blue ceiling adorned with yellow stars. The team immediately knew this was a place of royal prestige.

"The emotion of getting into these things is just one of extraordinary bewilderment because when you come across something you're not expecting to find, it's emotionally extremely turbulent really," said field director and University of Cambridge archaeologist Piers Litherland.

CONCLUSION

The acclaimed Egyptian intellectual and pyramid architect Ptahhotep said, "The greatest magic is the magic of knowledge." We have, over the course of this book, gained a lot of knowledge about the significance, beauty and accomplishments of Ancient Egypt. Despite the mist of uncertainty that hangs over this civilization – what elements are legend and what are real? – at least we have some sense of what it was like to have lived, breathed, worked, loved, worshipped and died in that unique time and place. We know how Egypt was born, flourished and fell, and what it has bequeathed our contemporary cultures and societies. We have adopted and built on some of its achievements while rightly abandoning those aspects that seem cruel and irrational to us today.

But is there more to learn from Egypt that might guide us through present and future difficulties? From the civilization's reverence for writers and

intellectual pursuits, its respect for nature, the opportunities it afforded to women and the empathy it showed towards animals, might future generations come to admire these things and use them to their advantage?

We will have to see!

FURTHER READING

Laura Andrews, *Ancient Egypt: The Definitive Visual History* (2021)

Jan Assmann, *Death and Salvation in Ancient Egypt* (2011)

John Baines and Jaromir Malek, *Cultural Atlas of Ancient Egypt* (1980)

Maria Betro, *Hieroglyphics: The Writings of Ancient Egypt* (2013)

Claudio Bocchia, *Tutankhamun, Nefertiti, Akhenaten and Amenhotep III – Pharaohs of the Solar Dynasty* (2024)

Eric H. Cline, *1177 B.C.: The Year Civilization Collapsed* (2021)

Hugo D. Cook, *Neon Squid and Sona Avedikian, Tales of Ancient Egypt: Myths & Adventures from the Land of the Pyramids* (2024)

Kara Cooney, *The Woman Who Would Be King: Hatshepsut's Rise to Power in Ancient Egypt* (2015)

Kara Cooney, *When Women Ruled the World: Six Queens of Egypt* (2020)

John Coleman Darnell and Colleen Manassa, *Tutankhamun's Armies: Battle and Conquest*

During Ancient Egypt's Late Eighteenth Dynasty (2007)

Terry Deary, Peter Hepplewhite et al., *Awesome Egyptians* (newspaper edition) (2023)

Zahi Hawass, *The Great Book of Ancient Egypt: In the Realm of the Pharaohs* (2023)

Barry J. Kemp, *Ancient Egypt: Anatomy of a Civilisation* (2016)

Barbara Mertz, *Temples, Tombs and Hieroglyphs* (2010)

Dominic Montserrat, *Akhenaten: History, Fantasy and Ancient Egypt* (2000)

Ian Shaw, *Ancient Egyptian Warfare: Tactics, Weapons and Ideology of the Pharaohs* (2019)

Ian Shaw and Paul Nicholson, *The Dictionary of Ancient Egypt* (1995)

Ian Shaw, *The Oxford History of Ancient Egypt* (2022)

Paul Strathern, *Napoleon in Egypt* (2009)

Helen Strudwick, *The Encyclopedia of Ancient Egypt* (2016)

Kasia Szpakowska, *Daily Life in Ancient Egypt* (2007)

The Three Initiates, *The Kybalion: A Study of the Hermetic Philosophy of Ancient Egypt and Greece* (1908; 2021)

Scott Trafton, *Egypt Land: Race and Nineteenth-Century American Egyptomania* (2004)

Richard H. Wilkinson, *The Complete Gods and Goddesses of Ancient Egypt* (2017)

Toby Wilkinson, *A World Beneath the Sands: The Golden Age of Egyptology* (2020)

Toby Wilkinson, *Ramesses the Great: Egypt's King of Kings* (2023)

Toby Wilkinson, *The Rise and Fall of Ancient Egypt* (2011)

Ann R. Williams (ed.), *Treasures of Egypt: A Legacy in Photographs from the Pyramids to Cleopatra* (2022)